HYDROPONICS

The Step by Step Guide for Hydroponics Gardening. Build your own Affordable and Sustainable Garden at Home, and start gathering Fruit and Vegetables. Start Growing any plant without the need of Soil in your Hydroponics Garden.

Michael Nestor

Table of Contents

INTRODUCTION

Hydroponics literally means "working water" (hydro=water, ponics=work). Practically, it means growing plants without using soil, delivering nutrients only by an aerated nutrient solution.

Hydroponics systems can be either closed or open systems. In closed systems the same hydroponic nutrient solution is recirculated and the nutrient content is monitored and adjusted.

Keeping the nutrient balance in such systems is a challenge and the hydroponic nutrient solution has to be sampled and analyzed every week. The nutrient solution composition has to be adjusted according to the results.

In open systems a fresh nutrient solution is introduced for each irrigation cycle.

Inert growing media are usually used in hydroponics. Unlike soil, that stores nutrients and directly interacts with the plant, the growing media used in hydroponics have little effect, if any, on the plant nutrition. As a result, the only source of nutrients is the nutrient solution, and therefore you have total control over your plant nutrition.

While soil allows more tolerance for inaccuracy, hydroponics leave very little room for errors. Because changes are rapid and mistakes can be very costly, hydroponics growers should make highly educated and accurate decisions.

Close monitoring of Water content is extremely important in hydroponics

Naturally, water plays a major role in hydroponics, making their quality and content - paramount.

There are several key questions that should be addressed when dealing with this issue:

Which nutrients are required? Are they all present in the correct concentration in your hydroponic solution?

What are the ratios between the nutrients? Do some nutrients affect the availability of others?

What is the total concentration of minerals in the solution?

Are there any harmful elements in the water? What is their concentration?

What is the pH of the hydroponic solution and how does it affect nutrient uptake by the plant?

First Step - Source Water Analysis

Hydroponics solution consists of minerals in the source water and the nutrients added with fertilizers. The choice of fertilizers type and amount added greatly depend on the initial content of source water. Therefore, testing the source water prior to preparing a fertilizer formula is imperative.

For example, your source water may contain a sufficient amount of calcium for your crop nutrition. In this case, you should not use calcium nitrate, not only because it is redundant, but also because any calcium addition might precipitate with other elements in the hydroponic solution, such as phosphorus, or interfere with uptake of others.

Additionally, source water may contain too large amounts of harmful elements, such as sodium, chloride, fluoride or excess of boron, rendering it unsuitable for hydroponics. This can be solved by pre-treating the source water with desalination or ion-exchange.

Source water analysis must contain at least the following information:

EC, pH, calcium, magnesium, chloride, sodium, sulfur and bicarbonate levels.

If your water source is a bore hole/well, it would also be wise to test for boron, manganese and fluoride levels.

The Essential Plant Nutrients

There are 13 mineral nutrients that are essential for completion of the plant's life cycle. Macro-elements are required in large quantities: nitrogen, potassium, phosphor, calcium, magnesium, sulfur. Micro-nutrients are required in very low concentration: iron, manganese, zinc, copper, molybdenum, boron, chlorine.

All of these nutrients should be provided in the hydroponics solution, in the right concentrations, and in adequate ratios.

According to the law of "limiting factor", if one nutrient is deficient, other nutrients cannot compensate for the deficiency, and the crop may suffer, resulting in decreased quality and/or yield.

Nitrogen, phosphorus and potassium

Most water sources contain only very small amount of these nutrients, if at all, therefore they must be provided using fertilizers.

Commonly used soluble fertilizers are MAP, potassium sulfate, ammonium nitrate, potassium nitrate.

Calcium and magnesium

These elements are usually found in source water, sometimes in adequate concentration for our needs, especially in well-water. If the concentration is higher than required, the source water should be pre-treated.

Calcium nitrate is the only fertilizer appropriate for calcium addition to hydroponics irrigation water. Magnesium nitrate and magnesium sulfate are both appropriate sources for magnesium addition. Note that calcium nitrate and magnesium nitrate also contribute nitrogen to the solution.

Sulfur

Sulfur is present in a wide range of concentrations in various water sources, and plants growing in hydroponics can tolerate relatively high concentration. But sulfur excess might have untoward effects and even limit nitrate uptake.

Micro-nutrients

Iron, manganese, zinc and copper can be provided in the sulfuric form, but their availability is greatly decrease in pH greater than 6.5. The chelated forms, may also be used, because they are available for uptake in a wider range of pH. Some growers regard EDTA as harmful for plants, and avoid its use.

Molybdenum is usually provided using sodium molybdate. The presence of sodium in this fertilizer should not be a cause for alarm. Because molybdenum is needed in minute quantities, very small amounts of this fertilizer are usually used, and the sodium addition is negligible.

Boron can be provided through boric acid or solubor. Solubor also contains sodium, but again, quantities are small enough as to not have a significant effect on sodium concentration in the solution. Range for adequate boron levels is very narrow (0.2-0.5 ppm) and can easily be missed, resulting in either deficiency or toxicity. Therefore, boron supplements should be carefully added. Well water often contain sufficient boron levels, so no boron addition is needed.

Harmful elements - Sodium - Chloride

Chloride is required by plants in minute quantities and most water sources contain chloride concentration well above and beyond plants require, so chloride deficiency is extremely rare. Chloride related problems are more commonly those of toxicities rather than of deficiencies. Therefore, using fertilizers which contain chloride is uncommon in hydroponics.

Sodium can be very harmful in recirculating systems, since it builds up with time in the hydroponic solution. Threshold concentration of sodium and chloride for most hydroponics grown plants is 75 ppm.

Electrical Conductivity (EC)

Electrical conductivity is a measure of the total salts dissolved in the solution (learn more about EC). It is used for monitoring daily applications fertilizers. Note that the EC reading doesn't provide you with information regarding the ratios between nutrients.

In closed hydroponics systems, with recirculating solution, nutrients which are not absorbed by the plants (such as sodium, chloride, fluoride etc.) or ions released by the plant, build up in the hydroponic solution. In this case you need more information about the solution content, that EC cannot provide. Frequent water analysis tests will help you decide on the timing for replacing the nutrient solution or dilute it with good quality water.

pH

The optimal pH range for the nutrient solution is 5.8-6.3. micro-nutrients are more available in lower pH, but when pH levels drop below 5.5, you run the risk of micro-nutrients toxicity, as well as impaired availability of calcium and magnesium. In hydroponics, especially in closed systems, the roots readily affect the hydroponic solution pH, so pH tend to fluctuate.

Appropriate products for acidifying the hydroponic solution are sulfuric acid, phosphoric acid and nitric acid. The preferred one is sulfuric acid because the EC control and pH control are kept separate. This makes the grower's job much easier.

Ammonium/nitrate is one of the major factors affecting the pH of the nutrient solution

Nutrient balance

Several nutrients compete with each other over uptake by the plant, so keeping adequate ratios is important for avoiding deficiency. For example, excess of potassium competes with calcium and magnesium absorption. A high iron/manganese ratio can result in manganese deficiency, and high sulfur concentration might decrease the uptake of nitrate.

As mentioned earlier, the nutrient balance in a closed hydroponics system changes frequently and has to be closely monitored and managed. Harmful minerals like sodium, chloride and fluoride build up in the solution and might reach toxic levels.

AQUAPONICS VS HYDROPONICS

Aquaponics:

Aquaponics, aquaponics farming or aquaponics gardening is a symbiotic method for growing plants and fish in a healthy, natural but soilless or near soilless environment for the benefit of everyone and everything involved. Not only will it produce healthy, tasty fruits and vegetables for your table, you can also choose to harvest the fish, an excellent and healthy protein source to complement the plants in your diet. It's up to you whether you would prefer the fish as pets or food, or a little of both.

The principle of aquaponics is simple: grow plants, fruit and vegetables in hydroponic conditions without chemicals by raising fish to provide the nutrients for the plants instead. Although the term "aquaponics" is recent and modern practices derive largely from research conducted in the 1960s, integrated farming of one type or another is probably as ancient as farming itself and may have evolved from the observation of symbiotic systems in nature. Whatever its origins, integrated farming has been practiced in Southeast Asian rice paddies for thousands of years. Fish in the rice fields help provide the nutrients for the growing crops and in turn the plants help keep the water clean for the fish.

Another example comes from the Americas: living on the shores of Lake Techotitlan and in dire need of arable lands, the ancient Aztecs of Mexico developed a technique to grow crops on floating rafts in near soilless conditions. Nutrient rich soil was dredged up from the lake bottom and spread on the rafts where the plants would grow. As the seeds matured into plants, their roots would penetrate through the soil and the reed rafts to the lake below where the fish were plentiful. Essentially the Aztecs were practicing large-scale aquaponics using the natural resources at hand.

Hydroponics:

What about hydroponics you ask? Modern hydroponics can be traced to 17th century Europe but there are arguments for much earlier origins.

The Aztec example discussed in the previous section is often cited as an early form of hydroponic farming, and it is a good example in the sense that the Aztecs were practicing near soilless farming, drawing nutrients directly from the water. The hydroponic element, in this case, was the plant subsystem. Other, more ancient examples that are often cited are the "hanging" gardens of Babylon, which are believed to have been fed with water drawn from the Euphrates river below. The theory is that some mechanism was employed to carry the water to the top of the gardens and the entire system was watered using a cascading or trickle down method to feed every plant in the chain. There is a catch, however, the system was not soilless or "hanging", according to descriptions by ancient writers (Diodorus Siculus, Strabo, Quintus Curtius Rufus, Philo of Byzantium). There may have been less soil than would occur in natural conditions but the descriptions make the terraces sound more like giant stepped planters with over hanging plants than hydroponic systems.

Ancient Egyptian hieroglyphics apparently describe the process of growing plants in water but there doesn't appear to be much information detailing what the process was exactly. Sometimes 1st century Roman Emperor Tiberius is credited with using hydroponic techniques to grow cucumbers out of season in proto green houses. This may be an argument for early greenhouses, but was it soilless? Finally, 13th century adventurer and trader Marco Polo came back from his trip to the Far East claiming to have seen plants growing on floating beds in China. It is not unlikely but whether this was an example of "pure" hydroponics or some form of aquaponics technology analogous to that of the Aztecs, is unclear. As we have seen the Chinese and other far eastern cultures were well acquainted with integrated farming and gardening.

All of this being said, and despite the scanty evidence, it would be very surprising indeed if ancient cultures had not experimented with growing plants in water or on water; examples of untethered, naturally floating plants are found in nature, why wouldn't they have tried it? The best evidence does appear to show, however, that the more successful models more than likely involved some form of aquaponics or integrated farming principles.

Why pick Aquaponics over Hydroponics?

Aquaponics and hydroponics are frequently described as competing models: you pick one or the other, but this is a false dichotomy. In reality, aquaponics is a form of hydroponic farming that can be traced back hundreds, even thousands, of years to ancient civilizations. It is a natural, chemical-free and symbiotic hydroponics model.

Even the terms used to describe them mean the same thing: hydro is the Greek form for water, aqua is its Latin form, both end with "ponic", which derives from the Greek ponos for labor or work. The terms, however, were coined relatively recently and have different histories: the modern term "aqua" ponic derives from a combination of aquaculture (fish farming) and hydroponics, hydroponics is just, well, hydroponics. This gives the impression that aquaponics is more recent and somehow is somehow derivative of hydroponics but as we have seen, if you factor in ancient practices, this belies the fact that aquaponics, or integrated farming, is probably ancestral to both modern versions.

Modern hydroponics takes the natural symbiotic element out of the equation and replaces it, for the most part, with a chemical solution. This may be necessary and viable for space exploration or other situations where a symbiotic system is impossible or impractical but otherwise, aquaponics is, in my opinion, the superior choice.

Both processes are highly successful at growing plants in soilless or near soilless conditions, so why pick aquaponics? Well, the absence of chemicals makes plants grown with aquaponics more flavorful and better tasting, plus, if you have a chemical sensitivity, then hydroponics may not be for you anyway. Also, if you are inclined to harvest them as well, the fish can be used as secondary food source. Basically by caring for the fish a few minutes a day you grow two excellent food sources for the price of one. The plants require little to no care if the fish are in good shape. Talk about efficiency! Some people get attached to the fish or are vegetarians and that is great, you still get perfect symbiosis: you feed the fish, the fish feed the plants, the plants feed you and filter the water for the fish, in an endless self-sustaining cycle.

Remember aquaponics is totally scalable: you can get started with a couple of plastic containers in your backyard or garage or turn the project into a large commercial enterprise and you still get experience a hydroponic system, a natural one. A simple system should pay for itself for itself in no time. With a little effort to get things started, you end up with a near-self-sustaining system that grows high quality, organic produce without the high price of store-bought organics. The satisfaction you get from growing your own food from scratch is a nice bonus too. Get the whole family involved and have fun with it. The components are relatively inexpensive and if you build it yourself you avoid the cost of a kit or hiring professionals to do it for you. If you have an interest in gardening or would like to have more choices regarding your everyday food sources, aquaponics is an alternative you might want to seriously consider.

CHOOSING A GREEN WALL?

Green walls are rapidly growing in popularity for their ability to bring the serenity of nature into the madness of our expanding urban environment - they naturally purify the air and have now been proved to reduce a building's heating and cooling costs. With so many options available it can be difficult to decide which kind best suits your needs but one of the first decisions you need to make is to whether to 'go hydroponic' or not i.e to use soil or not? I am biased towards one type in particular but my views may at least help you to ask the right questions before you buy.

Hydroponic Green walls - deliver nutrients to plant roots via water not soil. Small scale systems for domestic use can be relatively easy to maintain. However, larger hydroponic systems can be quite complex as well as more expensive to 'run' if they need professional maintenance. Here are a few factors to consider when trying to decide which way to go. If you 'think like a plant', the decision will be easy but maintenance rates as a big factor in my choice.

Water usage - A soil based green wall's natural ability to retain and evenly distribute water makes it more water conservative and much easier to maintain, especially if hand watering is an option. With hydroponic systems, a constant flow of clean, aerated water and nutrients is required to keep your plants healthy. The irrigation methods in large hydroponic systems can be quite complicated and require frequent expert attention. Pump failure without backup power could see plants lost in a matter of hours whereas a soil based green wall is more forgiving should irrigation stop, with a window of days for survival rather than hours. Another challenge you face with hydroponic installations is maintaining water temperature and pH levels which are extremely important, especially outdoors in warm climates. Changes in water temperature will affect your plants' ability to survive. A soil based green wall system consumes less water, does not have to use re circulated water and allows for more irrigation options which help to stabilize moisture levels and temperature of the soil.

Plant support and weight - Plants naturally produce incredible root systems to anchor themselves, whether this is on rocks, in soil or in synthetic materials like those found in hydroponic systems. One problem that can occur when using a hydroponic green wall system is that the plants may not create a strong enough root system to be sturdy and need weeks of 'training' to defy gravity. A soil based system with a large root space encourages the growth of an extensive, strong root system. The price you pay for this bonus though is that the system will probably be heavier than the hydroponic one overall so check that your wall/fence/deck can take it.

Nutrients and oxygen - Even expert botanists occasionally struggle with the proper balance of nutrients for their plants, regardless of whether these grow in soil or water. This is especially true in hydroponic systems in which a balanced solution of nutrients must be added to the water at specific times throughout the growth period. Even the smallest fluctuation at the wrong time can destroy your plants in a matter of days. Soil based green wall systems are much more forgiving in this area. The soil acts as a natural buffer and plant pantry, absorbing excess nutrients yet providing them to the plants as needed.

Another vital factor for success with hydroponic systems is the need for the right amount of oxygen at root level. Plants die of suffocation due to anaerobic activity caused by mismanagement of irrigation, nutrient mixes and microorganisms. In soil based systems, oxygen is supplied through a natural process - it becomes aerated by hardworking little microbes giving the roots the TLC they need.

Risk of disease - Combatting pests and disease is an ongoing problem for any gardener. Soil based green wall systems are more resistant to the spread of disease than hydroponic systems and can therefore be less risky. In hydroponic systems, where the plants' roots are more exposed to water that constantly re circulates, algae/bacteria can quickly travel to all plants via the system's irrigation superhighway. A disease called 'pythium' which causes roots to rot, is almost impossible to eradicate even with extensive disinfecting. Something as simple as unsterilized tools is enough to bring your hard work, as well as your emotional stability crashing down in a couple of days.

Power usage - Hydroponic systems require electric pumps that constantly re circulate water from a reservoir at the base to carry nutrients to all the plants. Due to the sensitive nature of a hydroponic system, a power failure could be devastating. With a soil based system, you have the option of regularly hand watering your plants with 'fresh' water and allowing the soil to carry the water throughout the system, reducing risk of water- borne disease. Timers and pumps can be used in soil based systems too but only intermittently as needed. Unless it's installed indoors where lights may be needed, hand watering your soil based green wall can eliminate the need for a power source all together.

Maintenance - Maintenance is one area where soil based green wall systems really shine. Some simple irrigation, fertilizer twice a year, some tip pruning and replacement of the odd plant now and again means you can spend more time enjoying your lushness than tending to it. The ongoing demands of cleaning parts and monitoring nutrient mixes for a hydroponic system are enough to scare some people off. Owners of large hydroponic systems usually hire a professional team to maintain their green walls which adds to the ongoing cost. Soil based green walls require much less maintenance since they're able to regulate water evaporation and nutrient delivery somewhat on their own.

While hydroponic green wall systems have their advantages, especially in large corporate settings, many people like me prefer the 'hands-on' nature of a soil based system. I think these are more cost-effective, easier to maintain, enable multiple uses and allow for the personal approach that gardeners know and love. After all, what fun is growing plants if you can't play in the dirt?

ADVANTAGES AND DISADVANTAGES

Hydroponics.

"The science of growing plants in a medium other than soil, using a mixture of essential plant nutrient elements dissolved in water."

Advantages and Disadvantages:

'Why bother with chemicals, tanks and such things, when all you have to do is put a seed in the ground, water it, and leave the rest to nature?' There are several answers to this question:

- no need to fertilize
- no cultivation
- no crop rotation
- virtually no weeds
- a tendency towards uniform results
- cleanliness
- larger yields
- less labor
- better control
- ease of starting new plants
- a means of upgrading poor plants

This list certainly looks impressive, but my personal experience backs up every claim.

No need to fertilize: There is nothing better for growing plants than a first-class soil. But what makes such a soil? Among many attributes, a good soil must have a balanced supply of available plant nutrients.

Many soils entirely lack one or more essential nutrient elements. Take phosphorous for example. This has often been supplied to the soil in a form of a fertilizer application of super phosphate. Similarly, potassium sulphate is used for potassium deficiency, ammonium potassium or nitrate or urea for nitrogen deficiency, and so on.

In the hydroponic method a balanced diet of plant nutrients is constantly available. There is no need to fertilize.

No cultivation: The back-breaking tasks of digging, raking or hoeing are virtually unknown in hydroponics. This particularly true of the coarser medium such as coarse sand or gravel. The voids in gravel provide all the soil atmosphere required by the plant. In fact with the sub irrigation technique in gravel, this atmosphere is replenished at least once daily. Part of the outstanding success of this method is due to the periodical supply of fresh air to the root system.

No crop rotation: There is no need to practise crop rotation in hydroponics. Lettuce, tomatoes or any other crop can be grown in the same place as the last crop, and as often as desired.

Crop rotation becomes necessary when the level of available nutrients in the soil, for a particular crop, falls below certain minimum limits. The hydroponic method per se precludes such an occurrence.

No weeds: Sterile media is used for growing, so soil-borne weeds are impossible to occur. If, by any chance, an 'air-borne' weed manages to land on your medium and get a footing, they are easily dealt with. This is gardening with one of its most annoying problems virtually gone!

Uniform results: This is a great boom for commercial farmers, who are, among other things, interested in getting uniform results in their production. Soils vary tremendously in both physical and chemical makeup. When using hydroponic gravel, and the same nutrient formulation, very uniform results are acquired.

Cleanliness: Many people fall victim to eating infected lettuce leaves. This is a real problem when animal excreta are used to enrich the soil. The US Army's hydroponics project in Japan was carried out specifically for this reason. Using sterile media and nutrient solution completely removes this problem.

Larger yields: Larger yields may definitively be expected, though some people expect extraordinary results from hydroponic gardening. If the 'yield' is defined as the return of mass of numbers of fruit, vegetable or flower per unit growing area per time, then the hydroponics method is superior. The reasons are not hard to see. Plants mature faster. Tomatoes for example, mature within 4 months from time of seeding. Lettuce take about eight to ten weeks. Secondly there is no competition by the plants for nutrients, so plants can be packed a lot closely together. With some crops, such as the tomato, it can be estimated that you can receive 3 to 4 times more than the yield expected in soil.

Less labor: Any businessman will tell you that labor is the most expensive item when manufacturing goods. The same is true of agriculture. There is digging to be done, fertilizer to be applied, and frequent irrigation. With hydroponics all three of those can be eliminated. It is completely possible to go away on holiday - return home, and pick the fruits or flowers from your hydroponic tank.

Better control: One of the many problems faced by gardeners is pH control. In the hydroponic system this problem is easily dealt with. Since inert growing media is used, it is a relatively simple procedure to change the pH of the nutrient to any desired level below 7,0. It is also comparatively easy to provide more or less nitrogen, phosphorous, potassium etc., should the plants require special treatment. With hydroponics this can all be arranged.

Ease of starting new plants: Growing seedlings in vermiculite is simplicity itself. There is no need to prepare special soil. Seedling will transplant with minimum of shock. Both these factors add up to the greater efficiency and ease for the gardener.

Upgrading poor plants: There is no finer way of revitalizing a poor plant than by transplanting it from soil into a hydroponic tank. Provided that there is no serious damage, a poorly growing plant may be transformed into a vigorous and healthy plant in the tank. It then may be transplanted into soil again if needed.

Of course, there have to be some disadvantages. Here are some of them:

On a large scale the construction of tanks and purchase of equipment such as pumps and reservoirs makes for a high initial outlay. This rather limits commercial growing to expensive floral crops and special vegetables fetching high prices. However, with the modern use of plastic lined tanks and overhead drip systems, this disadvantage falls away.

Some people state that hydroponics requires a bit of chemical knowledge. While it is true on a large scale it is helpful to have a knowledge of chemicals, for small scale and home hydroponics, many company's sell reasonably priced pre-made hydroponic nutrient solution powders, that you just need to mix with water. This eliminates the need for chemical knowledge, expensive scales, stocks of different chemicals etc.

MOST COMMON MEDIUMS USED IN HYDROPONICS

Since soil is not employed in hydroponic systems other substrates are required for flowers, herbs or vegetables to develop and provide an anchor for their root system. These growing mediums need to be inert so that they do not have an effect on the nutrients in the water solution. These mediums should also be pH neutral, have great fluid retention yet have capacity for air circulation and certainly be resistant enough to retain and support the plant. There are numerous kinds of mediums within the marketplace and the one that you employ will be determined by the types of fruits and vegetables you are wanting to cultivate. Just about any hydroponic retailers will be likely to recommend what substrates to employ, however I have provided an outline of the most popular substrates used in hydroponic methods.

Perlite

Is a kind of volcanic rock comprised of silica and commonly created by hydration of obsidian. There are different sizes subject to what you are growing. It is typically employed to grow cuttings in, and subsequently when the plants have grown to a particular size they may require another substrate to grow in based on the sort of hydroponic method you are employing.

Advantages

• Minimal price and low density material.

• Features good water retaining properties fantastic for potted plants.

• Features great drainage qualities and combines well with denser substrates.

• Ideal for establishing cuttings or seeds within it.

Disadvantages

• Not suitable for ebb and flow systems as due to its low weight it can shift or drift away during the flow periods.

• Not good for larger, weightier plants as it is unable to support and anchor plants roots properly.

Coconut Coir / Coco / Palm Peat

As the name suggests Coco is a product of coconuts, with all the outer shell of the coconut getting used after the coconut fruit has been taken out. It is treated to produce a kind of peat that is generally sold in brick shape. It is a good addition to hydroponic systems as it expands when water is added with about 6-8 times its initial size. It is robust enough for bigger plants and can last a lot longer than classic peat. Also it can be used as a form of soil even though it does not have any vitamins and minerals that soil has, yet it does provide you with a good structure in which crops can generate roots.

Advantages

• Excellent water retention yet allows air to move to the plants.

• Inexpensive environmentally friendly source hence kind to the pocket and to the planet.

• Can be combined well with different substrates for example perlite to improve drainage of water.

• Has natural anti-fungal qualities which aid to minimize flaws in plants.

• Has similar attributes to regular soil.

Disadvantages

• As mentioned above drainage will not be as good as some other mediums yet can be combined to reduce this problem.

• Can only be used a small number of times, however if you are altering your plant type in the hydroponic system it is a good idea to change your growing substrate also.

• Not completely successful in ebb and flow systems as some of the product can be washed away during the flow cycles. Yet is suitable for drip systems.

Clay Balls / Leca

These are small balls made out of clay that have been fired to maintain their form. They provide no nutrient value, are inert and have a neutral pH reading. These are perfect qualities to have in a medium as they do not restrict the nutrients added to the system. Due to these properties they are extremely popular with hydroponic growers.

Advantages

• Can be acquired in a variety of sizes so are appropriate for larger denser plants to supply good foundation of roots.

• Can be washed and recycled using white vinegar, chlorine or hydrogen peroxide solutions. Numerous hydroponic suppliers have washing solutions in store. Yet they need to be totally rinsed after washing or this can affect the plants in the next grow.

• Inexpensive to buy and make from a natural occurring material.

• Have superb drainage properties.

• Light to use but won't float away so can be used in ebb and flow systems.

• Holds moisture well.

• Can be blended with other mediums to improve drainage such as coco.

Disadvantages

• Despite the fact that they can be washed it not always advised as root growth can penetrate the clay balls. This can be evident upon breaking open the balls after use. This root development could impact future hydroponic grows.

• Does not keep moisture as well as coco peat but as mentioned above this can be reduced by mixing the two mediums.

Rock wool

Rock wool is also a favorite medium amongst hydroponic growers. It is a man-made product comprised of rock that has been separated into its mineral compounds and then spun to produce rock fibres. It is typically bought in brick or slab form and has a texture similar to those of fibreglass. It is typically used in small cubes to grow seeds or cuttings and enables the new roots to attach securely onto the medium.

Advantages

• Correctly treated and produced rock wool will be inert and therefore should not interact with other nutrients added to the hydroponic system.

• Proficient at retaining water essential for plant growth.

• Good drainage benefits.

• Easy for plants to take up nutrients and even provides some air circulation.

• Holds structure over extended amounts of time.

• Can be reused if washed however this is not typically advised.

Disadvantages

• Some lower quality rock wools are created from slag which can have a greater metal content. This can affect the pH of the wool and as a result impact on the nutrient absorption by the plant.

• It is a man-made material and as a result not as environmentally friendly as other substrates. It is more difficult to destroy and if placed and buried in land fill will not break down for long periods of time.

• As it has similar properties to fibre glass it can be carcinogenic, as the fibres can get into the lungs and might produce problems. It is recommended that you use a mask when originally setting up the rock wool within your system. The inclusion of water will decrease the fibre problem as they will be not as likely to become airborne.

NUTRIENT SOLUTION AND GROWTH ENHANCER

Most definitely, they are a must for successful Hydroponics. The reason is that with hydroponics, the media that is used is inert (soil-less) and does not contain any nutrient value for the needs of the plants. This means the plant(s) must obtain a balanced diet via a nutrient solution. Plant nutrition is complex, much like ours. A food pyramid for plants could be simulated to look like this: The lower portion of the pyramid, which is also the largest portion, would contain Nitrogen, Phosphorus & potassium. The next level on the pyramid, the middle portion, would contain Sulfur, Calcium & Magnesium. The third level going up the pyramid would contain Iron, Manganese, Copper & Zinc. And finally, the top level would contain Boron & Molybdenum. Sounds like a bunch of gobbly gook doesn't it? I'll try and simplify it by being more specific in explaining the different elements.

Plants require large amounts of nitrogen, phosphorus & potassium. These are primary elements and are known as macronutrients. Macronutrients also include the middle level on the pyramid; sulfur, calcium, & magnesium. They are secondary macronutrients as they are needed in a lesser amount than the plant needs for nitrogen, phosphorus & potassium. The remaining elements are considered as micronutrients or trace elements. They are still needed for healthy growth, but at a much lower amount than the others. All elements are found in the appropriate nutrient solution for your specific plant needs. Their roles in plant development are as follows:

Macronutrients - Major Elements

Nitrogen (N) - this element is part of all amino acids of chlorophyll & enzymes. It is absorbed in the form of nitrates or ammonium which the plants convert to proteins. Plants use nitrogen to produce new, lush growth. Symptoms of nitrogen deficiency are when older leaves turn yellow & die. If not remedied, the plants growth will be stunted with an unhealthy appearance - very few leaves.

Phosphorus (P) - phosphorus regulates root development, protein formation & cell division. It is essential to plant fruiting and flowering. When you add it as a supplement to your flowering plants, you will get faster growth with a lot more blooms. Symptoms of phosphorus deficiency are when the stems and the older leaves turn yellow; then, purplish discolorations appear on the leaves. The leaves may curl and die and the plants growth is stunted.

Potassium (K) - plants use this element to build cells and tissue. It is the most important element in flower and fruit development. This element, when used as a supplement, contributes to the plants hardiness which makes it more tolerant of changes in temperature & is more resistant to pest and diseases. Symptoms of potassium deficiency are when the edges of the leaves turn a rusty brown, leaves curl and turn yellow between leaf veins.

Macronutrients - Secondary Elements

Sulfur (S) - plants use sulfur to create proteins, hormones & vitamins. It helps plants to keep their dark green color. Symptoms of sulfur deficiency are when the plants growth is retarded, the stems are purplish in color and the younger leaves turn yellow.

Calcium (Ca) - plants need calcium to promote new root growth as it is an essential part of cell walls, enzymes and chromosome structure. Symptoms of calcium deficiency are yellow/brown spots on leaves. The leaves fail to fully expand.

Magnesium (Mg) - is an essential element that controls the plants ability to produce sugars from air and sunlight. It is also needed for the plants ability to take in their other essential nutrients and to make seeds. Symptoms of magnesium deficiency are when the older leaves turn yellow and become mottled with rust colored spots. Younger leaves may curl and crumble easily.

Micronutrients - Minor Elements (Micro or Trace Elements)

Iron (Fe) - is essential for photosynthesis. Plants must have iron in order to produce chlorophyll.

Symptoms of iron deficiency are when the new leaves look pale. The areas of the leaf between the veins are bright yellow while the veins stay green. The leaves and blossoms drop off.

Manganese (Mn) - acts as an enzyme activator to help form proteins and is necessary for chlorophyll formation. Plants wouldn't be able to carry out essential cellular functions without it. Symptoms of manganese deficiency are yellowing areas between the leaf veins while the leaf veins stay green.

Copper (Cu) - is an enzyme activator that assists in the process of photosynthesis. Copper contributes to the natural processes of plant metabolism and reproduction. Symptoms of copper deficiency are mis-shaped, yellow-spotted leaves.

Zinc (Zn) - is an integral component of many enzymes. It plays a major role in protein synthesis and is involved with the carbohydrate metabolic processes. Symptoms of zinc deficiency are yellowing of the leaves between the veins, smaller than normal leaves with distorted edges.

Boron (B) - plants don't need a lot of this element but it is essential for transporting sugars in the plant, for pollen formation & to grow new tissue. A symptom of boron deficiency includes new growth looking deformed and crumbling easily.

Molybdenum (Mo) - is needed to produce essential proteins via nitrate to ammonium conversion. Symptoms of molybdenum are yellowing leaves which are curled on the edges; deformed leaves which die and drop off.

Now that we know about macronutrients and micronutrients, how do we apply it to our hydroponics indoor gardening systems and in what amounts? This part is easy as there is a wide range of hydroponics nutrient solutions on the market. The nutrient solution can be purchased based on the type of plant, age of plant and stage of plant. This means that the nutrient solution is formulated to contain the elements needed for the specific plants needs during its growth cycles (blooming, fruiting, or for its age). When purchasing your hydroponics nutrient solution, be sure the label indicates that it is chelated meaning it has been chemically altered to ensure the nutrient solution can be easily absorbed by the plant(s).

The feeding regime is based on the needs of the plant and the hydroponics system you are using. The directions for use on the nutrient solution label and that of the hydroponics technique you are using will give you the information needed for successful plant growth and production.

So, you thought we were through. Nope, there is one more fact we have to take into consideration which is the pH balance of the nutrient solution. The correct pH level is critical for your plants ability to take in the nutrient solution for healthy growth. Fortunately, there are pH kits & meters that help us monitor the pH balance of the hydroponics nutrient solution. Due to pH levels fluctuating more rapidly in hydroponics, the nutrient solution should be checked every couple of days. Adjusting the pH balance is relatively simple. You can purchase pH up or pH down solutions and by following their directions you can raise or lower the pH level accordingly. To be proactive in reducing pH imbalances before you mix your solutions; test the water you will be using for your system and adjust the pH balance before mixing it with your nutrients. Also, never use hot water for mixing your nutrients. If rock wool is your medium of choice, you will need to soak it for 24 hours prior to use as it is inherently containing alkaline.

Is there more you can do to keep your plants happy?

With more and more people becoming educated in the health benefits of going green in their eating habits;

and, with the increased cost of vegetables, fruits and herbs at the supermarket; home hydroponics is becoming more popular. Anyone can grow hydroponically at home from a few indoor plants (flowering or not) to vegetables and herbs.

LIGHTING CONSIDERATIONS IN INDOOR HYDROPONICS

Lighting is of crucial importance to plant growth and plays a key role in determining plant yields. Hydroponics growing equipment manufacturers have, therefore incorporated a wide range of lighting system designs to meet specific requirements of different plants that are grown in indoor grow rooms.

Lighting requirements vary, depending mainly on the plant type, the area over which the plants are grown and the proximity of the plant to the light source. The most important consideration is the lighting level that a particular plant needs for healthy growth. Some plants like houseplants and ferns do not require as much light as salads and culinary herbs while tomatoes, orchids and flowering plants require the maximum amount of lighting. It has been observed that indoor growers typically tend to under-illuminate their indoor grow rooms as they try to cover too large an area with the available light. They need to understand the importance of adequate lighting bearing in mind that a smaller area that is adequately lighted will produce better results than a larger one with inadequate lighting.

Fluorescent Lighting

Fluorescent lamps are ideally suited for small scale salad and herb gardens and for the production of seedlings and cuttings. T-5 Fluorescent lights are suitable for slightly larger plants as the T-5 fluorescent bulbs are about equal in PAR value to a 400-watt Metal Halide light. These lights need to be kept close to the plants on all sides, but will grow fabulous plants with short internode distances as long as the plant are not too large. T-5's are best suited for vegetative growth.

High Intensity Discharge Lighting

Vegetables, flowers and several other plant varieties do best with all the light they can

get and the modern HID lights provide just what they need. HID lighting has developed with improvements in lamp and reflector design from a piece of equipment for specific needs to an almost "plug and play" use for the lay person. HID lights come in two designs - with remote ballasts and as integrated ballasts. The remote ballast design has the advantage of only its lightweight reflector unit needing to be suspended from the ceiling; the integrated design requires the full unit including the heavy ballast to be suspended.

HID lighting comes in two basic types- Metal Halide and High Pressure Sodium. Metal Halide HID lighting produces a blue white light, and has been recognized as especially well-suited for overall plant growth, while the High Pressure Sodium which produces a red/orange light is better suited to the flowering and fruiting period during which plants can more readily make use of it. Both types of HID lighting are in use with growers either alternating the two according to the plant growth cycle or mixing the two throughout the crop. However, the latest design of Sodium lamps which are now available in the "Agro" or "PLANTA" range can provide the light energy required during the entire cycle of plant growth and are being increasingly used by professional growers.

HID lights are available in wattage from 250 up to 1000 watts and beyond. The lamp which gives the maximum light output, watts used to lumens given is the 600-watt sodium lamp, producing 92,000 lumens.

Reflector

While it is important to use the right lamps to generate the right amount and type of light, it is equally important to ensure that the light is directed in a manner that ensures minimal wastage. Reflector design plays and important role in maximizing light utilization; a well-designed reflector can be as much as 30 % more effective than a poorly designed reflector in terms of its capacity to minimize light wastage. The most efficient reflectors now in the market feature designs generated using computer aided modeling techniques. These designs maximize light reflection onto the plants and enhance lamp life.

1. Light Movers

In addition to efficient light reflectors, rail systems that enable movement of lamp to ensure light exposure to the most remote plant go a long way in enhancing light utilization. A rail system called the Light Rail 3.5 has proved to be particularly effective in improving light utilization and should be considered by those who have a rectangular growing area. This is a simple device that uses a six-foot rail with a precision engineered carrier that moves the light back and forth over the growing area. The Light Rail 3.5 system offers several advantages- it covers a greater area and ensures that all plants receive the same amount of light; it eliminates having the plants moved around for light exposure and it eliminates shadows thus ensuring uniform plant growth. It also affords closer exposure of plants to light without burning the foliage. There are other systems that move the light along a circular path, these are more suited to square grow rooms. Some systems also allow combination lighting with a Metal Halide Lamp on one arm and a High Pressure Sodium on the other, or 4 different ceramic bulbs on 4 separate arms, each giving a different color temperature. These 4 different bulbs combine to make one very full spectrum when mixed via a circular or rotating light mover.

2. Reflected Light

Reflective surfaces around the growing area can make a difference in the amount of light that plants will receive. Poor reflectivity of the surfaces around a plant will diminish the amount of light as the surfaces will absorb most of the incident light. It is not difficult to ensure highly reflecting surfaces around the plants in a grow room. Walls can be easily painted with flat white paint, which is an excellent reflector. If this is not possible the walls can be covered with black/white plastic film which can also be used for the floor. Polystyrene foam sheeting can also be used as it is a good reflecting surface. The most reflective floor covering is brilliant white vinyl. It is tough and hard and makes an ideal reflecting surface. Finally, there is MYLAR, the most reflective material that can reflect 92 % of the light it receives.

3. Timers

Automatic turning on and off of the lighting system requires the use of an efficient timer. Incorporating a timer in the lighting system ensures that the plants in the grow room are exposed to light for the "on" set time after which the lights are switched off for the "off" set time. The continuous uninterrupted repetition of this on/off cycle is essential; a reliable, good quality timer is therefore important. It is best to avoid ordinary non-grounded plug-in timers as these are prone to failures causing disruption of flowering cycles in certain plants and increased power bills.

Power Consumption

Power consumption is one of the factors that need to be considered while working the economics of the project. However, this should not ordinarily deter the beginner as the

costs involved are surprisingly small. The beginner should work out the power requirement and its economics at the outset to avoid problems later.

Warning

Grow-rooms can be damp and humid. All electrical equipment, fittings and accessories should be carefully located to avoid any contact with water splashes. It is advisable to seek the help of a licensed electrician while installing the electrical system.

GROW BOX VS CONVERTING THE ROOM

There are numerous advantages to grow in your plants hydroponically in a grow box of versus converting a room in your house or apartment. Converting a room can be a huge undertaking. Often there will be a huge mess associated with converting one of the spare rooms of your house or a closet into a hydroponics grow space. Often these spare rooms on their own do not have adequate ventilation by default, so you could have temperature issues right off the bat.

Certainly in most cases it's not a good idea to have water directly on your carpet or wood floor. A grow box is self-contained unlike the grow room but the advantages don't stop there. A grow room cannot be moved in a moment's notice. A hydroponics grow box however can simply be moved to another room or space in your house or even to another growing location with ease. It comes completely assembled and ready to use. It can be broken down and cleaned in minutes. You can't rebuild the room that fast.

Let's take a look in depth at what would be required to turn say a stray closet in your house or a spare room in your house into a sufficient hydroponics of growing area for plants in multiple stages of growth. First of all, holes would need to be cut in the wall in order to intake fresh air and exhaust heated use air. You will need an odor removal system in order to keep your grow space odor free, and your exhaust bad smells and odors.

So you will need to think about good ventilation, such as very powerful fans to move plenty of fresh air in and out of your grow space, and plenty of powerful fans to exhaust air as well. Mini carbon scrubber's or ionizers to get rid that odor in line as well. Don't forget all those little accessories you'll need to get this project done that you probably don't have right now. Massive expense in tools and little parts.

Then of course you will need to build your own hydroponic system or purchase one. Hydroponic systems can be very expensive when purchased separately so you may decide to buy your own. This means a trip to a hardware store to buy lots and lots of little parts and tools so you can adequately. Think about how expensive those specific tools and various other devices that you'll need to make your own hydroponics system. It's getting complicated and expensive already. Unfortunately paying sales tax on a highly marked up products at your hardware store is more expensive than you originally estimated. Many people don't take that into account.

Not everything that you need is available in a hardware store. Some stuff only to be special mail-ordered from Internet sites like those pumps and all of the unique connectors for plumbing, not to mention the carbon scrubber you are certainly going to need. So now you're ordering from different vendors online again paying for shipping and a markup on more products that you're buying at full retail just to get a load of tools and boxes and generally a big mess at your home. You haven't even began working on your grow room yet look how much time and money you probably spent already at this point.

If you have a garage however you can move all that stuff out there that's makes building a grow box a lot easier when you have this adequate room. You'll need to spread all those parts out and figure out exactly how each part needs to be customized and joined together. You can find some good free grow guides online and follow these instructions carefully to make your own hydroponic system. Hopefully it will not leak. You probably will spend at least $40-$60 to find a decent book on constructing a hydroponic system, as these DVDs and grow both tend to be expensive and overpriced, but it is terrific information. That's why it commercial and not given away for free.

The lamps used in a good hydroponics setup are often the most expensive and critical part of your garden. This is what makes or breaks your grow. Often a good lighting system like 1000-watt high pressure sodium can cost as much as for $500 just for the lamp lighting system reflector with a ballast.

Once you do actually begin work drilling holes and making lots of noise and a huge mess in your hopefully soon-to-be garden. You may or may not built a decent hydroponics grow room. How much experience have you had doing this in the past? I hope you're not going strictly on what you just read online. The grow room versus a grow box will certainly not be portable. You can't get it out of there if you need to hurry.

I'm sure that your grow closet probably came out a little bit more amateurish than you may have had in your head. Unless you have experience wiring and working with wood and carpentry as well as with hydroponics, chances are you are not going to be very successful in your first few attempts at building your own grow space. This can lead to poor growing results, a lot of wasted money, a lot of room for improvement in future designs, and probably something you would do a little bit different if you had an opportunity to do it over again. Oh and then the big mess of a building and clean up.

Now let's take hydroponics grow boxes for instance and compare some of the key differences. They might look a little pricey at first, but are they really now you know the true cost of purchasing all those tools and small parts at full retail prices, and the time it took you to get all that stuff. A grow box usually has many years of design behind it, as these grow boxes are improved over time due to customer's feedback and new innovations from the company that manufactures the grow boxes is always updating their design.

So no matter what hydroponics you grow box you buy from the very small grow box all the way up to the midrange and large commercial scale grow boxes you know the design is pretty solid. Everything on the grow boxes work. The lights are designed to work with the ventilation system and keep the hydroponics grow box cool. The carbon scrubbers are already in place to get rid of the grow odors. The hydroponic system is built to fit perfectly into that space, and the whole unit can be moved anywhere you want in no time. Sometimes a hydroponics grow box even has wheels on it which makes it totally effortless to move. And when you add up the prices and your time now starting to look like a hydroponics grow box is a way better deal over building yourself.

Unless you're really the do-it-yourself type that has the confidence to be able to wire high amount of electricity around water which could cause a fire if done improperly, ask yourself is if it's really worth saving a little bit of money and potentially burning down your house. Chances are this is going to happen but a lot of people get themselves in trouble when their electrical system goes bad and they've done damage because they're not a qualified electrician.

Hydroponics grow boxes you know are designed to work exactly like they need to the very moment they show up. The grow boxes arrived fully assembled and literally just minutes away from plugging them in. Save yourself all the time and all the work and consider buying a commercial grow box which can be plugged into a wall and you are growing. And the technology that the hydroponics manufacturer has put into years of design the system to really make it easy for you to grow just about any plant you want the moment your grow box shows up.

GROW BOX HYDROPONICS SUGGESTION GUIDE

Advantage of choosing a hydroponics grow box manufacturer that produces custom built units versus one-size-fits-all variety.

Purchasing a hydroponics grow box is much like purchasing a car. When you purchase a car you do your due diligence. You do everything you can to read and research everything about your new car before you buy. You should be all over the Internet looking for reviews and articles, blog posts, research on forums and find out everything you can about that car before you buy it. You should definitely visit the manufacturers website multiple times and really study that car from top to bottom. You should memorize all this specification and attribute that car has. You know how fast it car can accelerate from 0 mph to 60 mph. You know how much gas that car use is on the highway and how much gas it uses on the road. And you definitely want to know how much horsepower that car has under the hood.

So why would purchasing a hydroponics grow box be any different? You definitely want to take the time to do the same amount of research on a hydroponics growbox that you would when buying a car because buying the right hydroponics grow-box certainly is a huge decision as well. If you're in the market for a new hydroponics growbox the first thing I would do is go to the website of the manufacturer of the grow box are interested in and study the specifications and the features of that grow box from top to bottom.

What you really want to do is familiarize yourself with the technologies and the features that are available in that in that specific growbox. Every hydroponics grow-box is a little bit different in terms of the features you are actually getting. Don't mistake the clean outer shell of growbox as being as simple as a box. There's a lot more to grow box than what meets the eye. A lot of grow box machines all look the same at first glance. Much like a car might look the same at first glance as most of them have four tires, windshields and a dashboard. But grow-boxes can contain very different components under the hood much as a car has. While in the case of a hydroponics growbox features you would look for is the amount of lighting and wattages used, the fans that are used and they're CFM rating, the size of the carbon scrubber installed on a growbox machines are all very important. These are all need to know specifications that you should memorize to make a good buying decision. Some manufacturers will try to rip you off by lower offering lower quality fans, or a small or nonexistent carbon scrubber that will do little to remove your grow odors. So if you really want to take the time to get to know the details of the website manufacturer as much as possible and really get to know the features and specifications of the hydroponics grow-box that you're interested in .

The next thing you would want to do is take a look at some other manufacturers grow boxes. Now what you want to do is to compare specifications closely. Take a look at the lighting systems for instance. How wattages and lamps matchup? Do the other manufacturers offer features such as vertically mounted fluorescent lights on their grow-boxes? Beware of manufacturers that simply offer one type primary HID lighting systems and not a variety of various types of lights. You also want to take a look at the size the fans and blowers used on the growbox system. If the growbox manufacturer is simply using inexpensive computer fans to cool the growbox you might want to check with other manufacturers to see if they are offering the same or more powerful fans within your price range. If a manufacturer is using large squirrel cage blower fan to keep their grow-box running cool that is a very good sign. Be sure to pay close attention to the differences in features, options, and fan, as well as lighting when comparing various grow boxes from different manufacturers to one another within your same price range

You should also beware of manufacturers that offer a one-size-fits-all variety grow-box. A lot of growbox manufacturers will try to sell you a hydroponics growbox with just a minimal amount of features and options. This means when you purchase your growbox you're lucky if you can choose more than they a CO_2 system and may be some extra nutrients go along with the system you are purchasing. Take a look if the grow box manufacturer offers features and options that you are really going to need into the future. Another thing you can look for when purchasing a grow box is whether the manufacturer offers a system that is totally automated, which takes out all the work of adjusting pH levels and adding water and nutrients your grow box system. This type of automation really gives you back a lot of your time and makes it a lot easier to use your new hydroponics grow box. I would definitely recommend a hydroponics grow box that is capable of maintaining itself. The next thing you would look for is whether or not various grow box manufacturers offer features such as air conditioning to keep your unit running cool. A lot of users will not get high success rates when growing indoors because of their grow boxes run too hot. What you're looking for is the manufacturer that offers air conditioning and very powerful squirrel cage blower fans to keep their grow-box systems running extremely cool at all times.

CONSTRUCTING A GROW BOX

Which is cheaper, buying a hydroponics growbox or constructing your own hydroponics grow box?

If you have spent any time on forums lately, you will notice that quite a few people recommend that beginners should build their own hydroponics grow box machine for their first grow. However, what does the beginner or amateur really know about building a hydroponics grow box? When you are about to take on an endeavor of building your own grow box, there are many safety concerns that you really have to think about. Really think about how much you really know about electricity and how to wire it properly. You will be dealing with a very high wattages and a dangerous amount of electricity in close proximity to water. Do you safely know how to work with electricity and high voltages around water? Do you have experience wiring for hydroponics applications? Do you know the difference between live wires and ground wires? Essentially at some point you will actually need a certified electrician to oversee your work in order to make sure that it is safe to run. Not doing so can lead to disastrous consequences that has happened for many poor growers.

Besides being a qualified electrician you really do have to know your stuff about ventilation in keeping your hydroponic grow box running super cool. You will be using very powerful lighting systems to light your hydroponics grow box machine. You can be using 600 Watts or even 1000 W lamps in order to light up your grow box machine. These types of lamps are known to generate an immense amount of heat. Many people talking on the forums will recommend building your hydroponics grow box out of some sort of particleboard or cheap painted wood. This is a really bad idea! Danger! Danger!

I have seen a lot of posts where users will recommend to beginners that they build their hydroponics grow box out of inexpensive cabinets made for clothes and built out of wood furniture found at hardware shops like at Home Depot for instance. Can you imagine how dangerous it is to put high-powered 1000 W lamps inside of a wood closet that I was meant for clothes and is nothing more than particleboard. Not a good material to build a growbox out of. Unless you really know what you're doing. Wood is about the worst possible materials to use when building your own hydroponics grow box. I would really recommend using metal. However, metal is much harder to work with. Another reason for buying it from the professionals. A good grow box should be built out of metal for safety and durability. Metal is very difficult to work on and hard to do on your own.

There is no way you can get into bigger trouble than by having your hydroponics grow box catch on fire, can be a problem when built from a wood cabinet from hardware store. Fire is a common amateur mistake which happens more often than you know when you talk about mixing high amounts of electricity and water together in a very small space or enclosed space such as in a wood cabinet. Often to try to save money beginners and those on a budget will not use adequate fans to keep their grow box system running cool. Very powerful fans are in order to keep your grow box running cool because heat will damage your plants. Those fans also have to be set up in a very specific configuration in order for them to work correctly. In order to get a very successful yield you really have to know quite a bit about the ventilation to get the very best plant growth is a grow box and avoid starting a fire in one that you build on your own.

Often members of the forum that suggests building your own hydroponics grow box forgets to mention a lot of stuff that is needed to build a successful growbox machine from scratch. Sometimes you will see post from users on a forum claiming that you can build a grow box for much cheaper than what commercial grow box manufacturers sell their products for. Is that really true? Do we believe everything we read on a forum? How do we know the qualifications of those posting the messages? People like to talk the talk but can hardly walk the walk on forums. Obviously some do know what they they're talking about, but you have to be an expert yourself to know the difference between those qualified and those not qualified to give suggestions on how to build your own grow box. There is a lot of incorrect and misleading information floating around on his forums like wildfire.

These types of comments about building your own hydroponics grow box at such cheap prices is completely ridiculous when a hydroponics manufacturer is purchasing parts for their inventory or purchasing directly from the manufacturers, in most cases in case quantity and getting wholesale lowest-prices which you're not getting! When you're buying one off parts from a hardware store you are paying full markup a very high rate. You are not getting any breaks whatsoever on any of the equipment you buy when you purchase from a hardware store one at a time in small amounts. You are paying a tremendous markup for everything you buy plus you are also paying tax and wasting gas.

Besides there are hundreds of little parts that simply slipped your mind that you will actually need to build their own growbox like junction boxes, lighting systems and reflectors, ballasts and pumps, just to name a few. You will pay top dollar for all of these necessary part. But the expenses really don't stop there. On top of that I'm sure there's a lot of tools they really need to use to build your own hydroponics grow box which you probably don't already own. You will need a variety of types of drills, saws, cutters, and all types of lighting and an electronics like timers to be able to build the proper hydroponics grow box from parts from the hardware store.

Oh and not to mention, besides the tools you'll need all the attachments that go along with these tools which can be very expensive when purchasing from Home Depot or Lowes. Maybe if you're lucky you'll own a few of these tools but certainly not all of them, and certainly not the proper attachments in the proper sizes. So now instead of just buying little parts you're buying all the tools to all the accessories at full retail prices. Will you have a use for all these tools you used on building your hydroponics grow box at a later date? I certainly hope so because they cost you enough money!

Now you've got a whole garage full of parts and you will need to figure out how to put them together from scratch based on sketchy plans found online. Also consider how much is your time worth? This type of project can take quite a while to construct. Sometimes it can take days for simple design two weeks or months or more complicated. Do you really know that your design works? Have you built one of these grow boxes before? How qualified are the people on the forums that are recommending certain configurations of boxes they build? Why is there area of expertise? How many grow boxes have they built and what makes them qualified to give advice on building a grow box? Do not follow the guidance of someone with limited or questionable experience who has posted anonymously on a forum? It's really hard to know what the actual qualifications are of someone when you actually know nothing about them. That is why you have to take what you read on the forums with a grain of salt.

Now let's consider purchasing your own hydroponics grow box from a reputable manufacturer that has been building grow box machines for many years and has a lot of experience. Keep in mind that this is a business for the business who is involved in making hydroponics grow boxes every day. Everything they do all day long revolves about around building the best grow boxes they can.

They have done a whole lot in research and development to come up with the current designs they utilize in their products. If you're a professional growbox manufacturers you get a lot of feedback from customers that purchased the machines and the they can make suggestions for improvements on future grow boxes designs. Not to mention professional grow box manufacturers have been manufacturing a product for a while and know their products inside and out. You can naturally see how much a grow box can be improved when you have feedback from hundreds of users of a particular manufactured product. So naturally when you are purchasing from a reputable hydroponics grow box manufacturer you are getting a well-built product from an expert in their industry.

When you take the time to build your own hydroponics grow box there is no guarantee that you're going to get it right the first time. But when you purchase from a reputable hydroponics grow box manufacturer chances are the growbox that you're going will work fairly well just based on the company it came from. You know that it will be safe to handle the amount of light that is used in the growbox because the manufacturers know what types of fans to use to keep the growbox machines running cool and safe.

You know the wiring in that professionally built grow box is going to run safely because the electrical wiring had been done by qualified electrician. When you purchase a growbox versus building your own grow box there'll be no mess. Typical growbox manufacturers will send out their units completely assembled and ready to grow the day you get them. So when you purchase a professionally built hydroponics grow box chances are that it will actually be quite a bit cheaper than building your own when you consider all the money you save on those little tools and all the little parts plus the time all combined together a grow box purchase will cost a lot less money than building your own, and will be guaranteed to work.

It's my opinion that there's little to no advantage to building your own hydroponics growbox unless you are an expert with electrical, metal working, working with wood, and know the science of hydroponics inside and out. Those types of individuals that already use tools and have types of qualification could probably build a really nice grow box on their own. For the rest of us that have little to no experience in the various fields required I was definitely recommend you play it safe and go with the pre-build hydroponics grow box is sure to work and be safe to use.

However, if you still want to attempt building one of your own I would suggest taking a look at the video on this hydroponics website. They have some of the best growboxes that I've ever seen, and their design look rock solid. If you want to attempt to make one on your own make it like these guys have. They really know their stuff. Or better yet think about purchasing one and saving your money. But it's really entirely up to you when you want to do. I just thought I'd throw out some of the common mistakes that newcomers have posted on forums about in the grow boxes gone wrong in the past.

WHAT ABOUT GROW BOX DEALERS?

Beware of dealers posing as manufacturers when purchasing your first hydroponics grow box.

So, you want to begin growing indoors. You have decided to purchase your first hydroponics grow box and grow your own. You are no longer willing to pay the high prices for fruits and vegetables sold by companies like whole foods and he decided to grow your own fresh fruit and vegetables right in your own home with hydroponics. By no doubt you've taken the time to do the research and decided against building a room for hydroponic since this is such a messy and expensive endeavor.

Since you're in the market for a new hydroponics grow box there is something that I would definitely look out for before you make any purchase. There are other in reputable dealers out there that are posing as manufacturers of hydroponics grow box systems. They will often have the same photographs on their website as the actual real manufacturer of the hydroponics growbox you are actually interested in. They will often put misleading information on the website making it look like they make the machines they sell, but they do not actually manufacture the machines they sell.

Dealers are middlemen and not the direct manufacturers. Dealers are in business to make a quick buck and get out. Customer service means little to in reputable grow box dealer. When you call to ask sales questions and technical support questions you are speaking to somebody that is not truly familiar with the products they sell as they do not build the grow boxes themselves, and often they will give you misleading and inaccurate information on the product you are calling about. The point I am making to you is that dealers do not know their products as well at the manufacturer of the product and dealers will often give you wrong or bad by information or specs that can lead to a lot of trouble in the future.

If you were to actually deal with the manufacturer of the grow box you are interested in purchasing, the chances are you will be able to get a much better deal. The manufacturer of the grow box has much more room to go down on price than a dealer and can often make exceptions and deals that no dealer was not capable of doing. Dealers don't have control over their fixed price and can rarely match the deal you can get directly from the manufacturer. Also when you speak to the direct manufacturer of the growbox versus simply dealer of the growbox you are virtually guaranteed to be getting correct information on the product you're thinking about purchasing. The sales people that work at the actual manufacturing facility of a hydroponics company knows their product lines inside and out. When you speak to a sales representative from the manufacturer you are almost assured with 100% certainty that the information you are giving you is correct and accurate about the grow box that you are interested in purchasing.

If something ever goes wrong with your growbox or even during the purchasing and building portion of your grow box, you really are up the creek without a paddle when purchasing from a dealer versus real manufacturer. If anything were to go wrong with the transaction the dealer can do little to help you unlike the manufacturer who has much more control. When purchasing from a dealer versus purchasing from a hydroponics grow box manufacturer you risk that something could go wrong that the dealer has no control over, and you get stuck holding the short straw on the deal when the dealer and the manufacturer tried to work it out.

It's even possible to pay a dealer for a growbox product and for whatever reason the dealer is delaying in sending money to the hydroponics grow box manufacturer for a few weeks, which could delay your unit shipping out! Many dealers that pretend to be hydroponics manufacturers are often the only dealers with no heart that use your money to purchase advertising and make money off you to real in more victims. That means that when you purchase of a grow box and send in the cash it might not even go to your grow box. Often dealers will rely on people purchasing grow boxes right now to those that already purchased in the distance past and you are actually paying for their machines. I would not be happy about this If was purchasing a machine.

For technical support and that product descriptions you definitely always wanted deal with the manufacturer of the hydroponics grow box and not simply a dealer of the grow box. This way you'll get the best prices when you buy a multiple-unit, as well at the best technical support and product information possible.

If something ever should go wrong, you much better off dealing with the manufacturer directly rather than a distributor who might be gone tomorrow or in your time of need. Distributors rarely think about their customers when the deal goes wrong. Distributor of hydroponics growboxes have little commitment other than the website in the industry they are selling in just salesman who can sell vacuum cleaners one day and use computers the next.

Dealers disguising themselves as manufacturers often has many websites selling many different products and know very little about anything they sell including the hydroponic industry in general which you really need to be an expert on.

Be sure when you purchase a hydroponics growbox they you are getting it from the actual manufacturer and not some shady dealer who artificially raises the prices to try to rip you off. Don't be fooled by these guys; they are just in it to make a quick buck and leave you holding the bag. When purchasing a hydroponics grow box do your research and make sure your purchasing from the actual grow box manufacturer and not from some grow box dealer who is trying to pose as the actual manufacturer to fool you in addition to rip you off, and charge you more!

PLANT GROWTH

PLANT GROWTH & PHYSIOLOGY.

There are three classes of plants. Each of these classes metabolize in a different way. The first class are succulent plants called CAM. These plants like low light and high humidity levels and so thrive indoors, in bathrooms and kitchen areas.

The second class of plants is called C4. These plants grow in hot arid regions and are very efficient at using both Carbon Dioxide (CO_2) and Sunlight. Most C4 plants are grasses.

The third and last class of plants are called C3. These plants join two 3-Carbon atoms together to produce sugar. The chemical formula for sugar is $C_6H_{12}O_6$ which is 6 Carbon, 12 Hydrogen and 6 Oxygen atoms stuck together. Most of our favorite plants are to be found in this class.

HOW DOES A PLANT WORK?

Like all living things, plants breathe 24 hours a day. In order to make energy each plant cell respires (converts plant sugar to energy). The plant uses Oxygen (O_2) and expires, or breathes out, Carbon Dioxide (CO_2).

In the same way that energy moves around the human body, so water, nutrients and plant sugars are continually being transported around the plant body. The leaves create a circular flow with the roots. This circulation occurs when the leaves draw up, water from the roots, through their Xylem.

These are straw like cells found in the plant stem. The water continually evaporating from the leaves sucks up more water from the roots and creates the internal water pressure that keeps the plant rigid. Thus if the plant is deprived of water, as in a drought, it loses its rigidity and begins to wilt when the internal pressure drops.

The leaves return energy to the roots in the form of sugar solutions. These are transported from the leaves via the plants Phloem. These are also straw like cells found in the plant stem. In this way the leaves exchange sugars for water and nutrients, while the roots exchange water and nutrients for sugar solutions. This liquid circulation is constant and continuous throughout the life of the plant.

THE MAIN PLANT PARTS.

The 3 main parts of a plant are the Roots, the Stems and the Leaves. Each of these parts is of great importance and any problem that arises in any of them will be a major one. The most sensitive part is the roots, as well as being the most difficult to see should a problem occur.

The Roots:

The miracle of growth starts at the roots. As already mentioned, roots transport nutrients up to their leaves and plant sugars are returned by the leaves. The roots also act as storerooms for the excess sugars that are produced by the leaves. These sugars are stored in the form of starch. The size of the root ball and therefore the amount of starch that can be stored, determines the success of the plant in terms of growth and productivity.

The size of the root system is directly affected by the amount of moisture, the temperature, the available Oxygen and the supply of plant sugars being transported down from the leaves. According to Graham Reinders, in his book "How to Supercharge Your Garden", a research Rye plant in a 12-inch pot was said to have had 14 billion root hairs. These hairs would have stretched 6200 miles (nearly 10,000 km) if placed end to end and covered an area of 180ft by 180ft (about 55m by 55m). The greater the root system is the more energy (starch) it will be able to store and so, the more nutrients it will be able to send up to nourish the leaves. The plant will then have the capability to grow stronger. The end result of this is that the leaves will be able to pass more plant sugars back down to the roots and so the cycle continues.

Another factor to be taken into account is the root medium. Plants take their nourishment from the medium surrounding their roots. It stands to reason that the less energy the plant has to expend in order to get that nourishment the more energy it will have available to use for growth and nutrient exchange with its leaves. Because a plant takes most of its water in via its roots, (the root hairs trapping the water molecules surrounding it) and transpires about 99% of that water out via its leaves, it will wilt and fall over if its roots cannot extract enough water out of its surrounding medium.

A plant growing in the ground will take its moisture from the surrounding soil. This moisture normally gets into the soil as rain and the plant absorbs that rain and the nutrients that have dissolved in it, via its root hairs. After the rain has stopped the topsoil quickly dries out as the water filters into the ground. Because of this drying out the plant has developed a means of absorbing Oxygen via its upper roots. The top third of the roots become specialized as "Air Roots" while the bottom third becomes specialized as "Water Roots".

It is vital to ensure that the Air Roots are not kept constantly wet as this will result in the plant drowning. The Water Roots however, may be kept wet all the time, providing that the water has sufficient Oxygen dissolved in it. Insufficient Oxygen will result in roots with brown, discolored root tips and subsequent infections. Healthy roots are a crisp, white looking structure.

The plant is quite capable of healthy living with the roots exposed to light as long as they remain moist. However, light will encourage the growth of Algae which will cause odors. The Algae will also compete with the plant for Oxygen during the dark periods and nutrients in the light ones. This, of course will mean the plant has to work harder in order to produce sufficient sugars for its needs. The Oxygen produced during the dark periods is used to help the roots convert these sugars, from the leaves, into energy (Starch).

PLANT NEEDS

What Do Your Plants Need?

All plants need the correct conditions in order to grow to their full potential. Plants grown using hydroponics systems are no exception to this basic rule. Like their soil grown cousins they need sufficient light of the correct wavelengths, a suitable temperature, an adequate water supply, enough oxygen, mineral nutrients and support for their structures.

Sufficient light of the correct wavelengths, used by the plant at the growth stage it has reached, is essential for its survival. Plants use lots of light, at least 8 to 12 hours each day, in order to make carbohydrates from CO_2 and water. Chlorophyll, the green color in plants, absorbs the sunlight and uses its energy to synthesize these carbohydrates. This process is known as photosynthesis and is the basis for sustaining life in all plants. Because animals and humans get their food by eating plants, it can also be said to be the source of our life. Artificial lighting is generally a poor substitute for sunshine, because most indoor lights provide insufficient intensity to produce a mature crop. High intensity lamps such as high-pressure sodium lamps can provide more than 1,000 foot-candles of light. The hydroponic gardener can use these lamps very successfully in areas where sunlight is inadequate. The fixtures and lamps, however, are usually too expensive to be viable for a small commercial operation. It is important to allow adequate spacing between plants as this will ensure that each plant receives sufficient light in the grow-room. For example, tomato plants, pruned to a single stem, should be planted so as to give 4 square feet per plant, while European seedless cucumbers should be allowed 7 to 9 square feet and seeded cucumbers about 7 square feet. Lettuce plants need to be spaced 7 to 9 inches apart within the row and 9 inches between rows. Most other vegetables and flowers should be grown at the same spacing as recommended for a conventional garden.

A suitable temperature is required for the plant to grow normally. Temperatures that are too high or too low will give rise to abnormal development and reduced production. Summer vegetables and most flowers grow best between 60° and 80° F, while winter vegetables like spinach and lettuce prefer temperatures of between 50° and 70° F.

An adequate water supply is not normally a problem when using a hydroponics system, since the basis of hydroponics is the supply of water containing nutrients in solution. Having said this however, there are some systems which can give rise to inadequate watering, with the consequent detrimental results to your plants. Ebb and flow systems which are not checked on a regular enough basis, can run short of nutrient in their supply tanks, as can continuous flow systems. Most, if not all, automated hydroponics systems can have disasters if they are not monitored closely. A blocked or burst pipe, or a pump failing can result in lack of nutrient flow, which, coupled with the intense lighting and the correct ambient temperature in the grow-room, will result in dry roots and severe damage to, or even the death of, your plants.

Oxygen is a basic requirement of most living things. Plants need oxygen for respiration, so that they can take up water and nutrient. In soil systems enough oxygen is usually available, but plant roots growing in water will quickly use up the supply of dissolved oxygen. This can damage or even kill the plant unless additional air is provided. A common method of aerating the nutrient is to bubble air through the solution. Continuous flow and aeroponic systems do not usually need supplementary oxygen.

Mineral Nutrients are needed by most green plants. They must absorb certain minerals through their roots in order to survive. In conventional horticulture these minerals are supplied by the soil and by the addition of fertilizers such as manure and compost. Nitrogen, phosphorus, potassium, calcium, magnesium, and sulphur are needed in large quantities, whilst the micro-nutrients, iron, manganese, boron, zinc, copper, molybdenum, and chlorine are also needed, but only in very small amounts.

Support is normally provided by the soil that surrounds the growing plant. A plant grown using hydroponics however needs to be artificially supported. This is usually done with string or stakes. It is possible to buy inexpensive automatic string reels to support your plants as they grow. This cuts out the tedious task of having to keep re-adjusting the strings on fast growing plants.

ENVIRONMENT

The Success or Failure of Your Plants Depends On Their Environment.

The environment, or climate, in which your plants are grown is one of the most important factors affecting your end results. The temperature and humidity have to be right for the type of crop you are raising, the lighting has to be of sufficient intensity and duration for the stage your crop has reached. These and many other factors have to be considered before you can hope to grow a healthy and productive crop.

Let's look briefly at the various factors involved. Growing plants indoors means that you have to create similar conditions to those outside. This may seem obvious at first glance, but is it true? Ask yourself what the advantages of Hydroponics gardening are. The outside climate is very varied and does not always work to the plant's advantage. For example, a bad storm or a late frost can damage or kill tender young plants.

One of the major advantages of hydroponics gardening is that you can control the climate within the grow room. This means that you can supply your plants with the ideal conditions for their healthy growth, throughout their lives. This ensures a good healthy yield and a bigger profit margin.

So what do you need?

Having decided upon which type of hydroponics system to use, you now need to promote the right growing conditions. All healthy plants require a good supply of water and balanced nutrients. They need the right kind of light, for the right period of time, each day. Your plants will need some kind of support for their structure, especially as they mature and grow heavy with harvestable produce. Like outdoor plants they also need the temperature to be within a certain range. Too cold and your plants will not thrive, but remain poor stunted things. Too hot and they may well dry out, then their leaves will wither and the plants die.

The addition of Carbon Dioxide gas (CO_2) may be advisable to promote Photosynthesis within the green leaves of your plants. Finally, some form of clean fresh air circulation is needed to ensure that your crop can breathe. Like you, your plants need Oxygen for life. They breathe it in through their tissues and like you, can become sick if it is dirty or contaminated. So, taking these factors one at a time, how can we create the optimum conditions for our plants?

Firstly, water and a good supply of balanced nutrients are essential. Which nutrient to buy and how to use it? This again is a major question to some people. My advice to you would be to go with a nutrient that you can understand and are comfortable using. As you gain experience and confidence you can experiment with other methods and suppliers at will.

Lighting is another key area that seems to cause newcomers a problem. The type of light and the number of daylight hours are determined by the species of plants you are cultivating and their stage of development. Young seedlings and cuttings, for example, need much softer light than do plants about to flower. Equitorial plants will generally need a higher light intensity for a longer period than will plants from the regions where days and growing seasons are short. Ask your hydroponics supplier for help in any of the areas you are unsure of. He will be pleased to assist you.

When looking at lighting you also need to take into account the area to be covered and whether the lights are to be static or moving.

A Brief Word of Warning:

Poor quality lighting systems can be very dangerous and accidents are more likely to occur if the person who sets up the equipment is not particular about safety. Always buy quality assured electrical equipment that carries the safety mark for your country. Do not risk your life or the lives of those you love just to save a few pounds or dollars.

IF IN DOUBT CONSULT A PROFESSIONAL ELECTRICIAN

Plants can be supported in a variety of ways, by using frames and tying the plant stems to them at regular intervals using plastic ties. Automatic reels can be bought which makes the job a lot easier. They consist of a spring loaded reel of cord with a hook arrangement that fixes to the ceiling, or a top runner, and a hook or loop to tie to the top area of the plant stem. As the plant grows so the slack in the cord is taken up by the reel. Depending on your growing system the roots will either be supported or not. If no support is used, for example in a water culture system, then the plant should be supported at or near the base of the stem, to stop it lifting if reel supports are used.

And so to the temperature control in your artificial climate. The optimum temperature for your plants will again vary with both genus and species. Ask your supplier what this should be. Now you will need devise a system to maintain the temperature within the optimum top and bottom limits. This can be achieved by either a series of fans and/or heaters together with various other pieces of equipment such as timers, controllers, monitors and CO_2 dosers, or by a commercially produced environmental control system. These ready-made systems come in a variety of price options designed to suit almost every pocket.

In general, the more you are prepared to spend, the more sophisticated the systems that are available to you. Fresh air requirements for your grow room are normally provided using a fan assisted ducting system. This introduces clean air from the outside, via a filter to remove impurities. An Ozone generator is often used to improve the supply of oxygen and neutralize any noxious odors. Another similar ducting system then extracts the dirty air back to the outside, again via a filter to remove impurities and cut down on unwelcome odors. Humidifiers can be used, if needed, to increase the amount of airborne water vapor.

THE AUTOPOT

The Advantages of the Autopot System

The basic Autopot System consists of a plant pot on a membrane in a container. This container has a SmartValve built into it which is fed from a nutrient tank.

As the plant in the pot uses nutrient the level of nutrient in the Autopot container is maintained by the SmartValve. This means that the plant always has the optimum level of nutrient at its disposal. As the plant grows and needs more nourishment, the SmartValve opens more frequently to replenish the nutrient supply from the tank. Because the plant pot is sat on a membrane, it will only take up what it needs in the way of moisture. This system ensures that the plant does not become too wet and drown or rot, neither can it dry out provided that the tank is kept topped up.

In our climate in the United Kingdom, where rainfall is often quite high and sunshine limited, I have found that the results obtained with the Autopot system have far outstripped those of a conventional system of soil and a growbag.

These results have only been studied using tomatoes, however I have no doubt that the same benefits would apply to virtually any type of plant.

I have grown a crop of tomatoes from seed this year and for the first time tried the Autopot system against a growbag and against pots hand watered with nutrient solution. The substrate used was washed coco. The seedlings were grown on to about 4" in height using rockwool cubes and a small propagation tray. They were transplanted into 8" pots (3 plants per pot.) and the pots placed in either Autopot systems or into containers about 2" deep. Some were planted in soil in Growbags.

The Autopots were connected to a nutrient tank and the trayed pots were watered twice daily using nutrient from the same tank. The plants in the Growbags were watered daily and had plant food added to the water as directed on the container. It was found that the Grobag plants did not grow as well as the others and fruited less abundantly.

The plants in pots and container trays fruited well, but during hot spells needed more frequent watering as the coco does not retain moisture. By far the best results were obtained from the Autopots. The plants grew quickly and were soon very well established.

The root balls soon became dense and well formed. Within a short time, the plants became sturdier than there less fortunate siblings and started to flower.

I had deliberately done no maintenance with any of the plants. they were planted, fed and left to grow without interference. This meant that the crops would be smaller than if I had pinched out the shoots, but there could be no discrepancy due to better maintenance. The results were quite staggering. The trayed plants produced some 250% - 300% more fruit than the Growbags and the Autopot had at least double the crop produced by the trayed plants.

The only drawback with the Autopot was that when it rained the water ran back into the nutrient container causing it to overfill. This problem did not seem to be detrimental to the plant's growth or yield.

HARD WATER

Your Water Hardness is a Critical Factor for Success.

What Is Water Hardness and Why Does It Matter?

Water Hardness refers to the alkaline mineral ion count, usually from Calcium Carbonate and bicarbonate. Water with a high count is called Hard Water. You can usually tell if you are in one of the many hard water areas of Europe because your kettle will get a buildup of 'Lime scale' on the inside.

Hardness of water can be measured in parts per million by using a total alkalinity test kit. These cheap simple test kits are available from your local hydroponics retailer and are quite accurate enough for the purpose. If your water tests at anything over 150ppm it should be considered to be hard. Do not be alarmed if your water is hard, it does not mean you cannot grow things using hydroponic methods.

Why Does It Matter If My Water Is Hard?

For many years, growers in some areas have had unacceptable results, with low yields and poor plant performance. The reasons for this have been unclear until it was realized that the plants were suffering from a chemical imbalance. Hydroponics growers were particularly badly affected in these areas.

Growing hydroponically using normal nutrients means adding a balanced solution of chemicals to the hard water. The hard water already contains an excess of some of the essential minerals that the plant needs and so the solution quickly becomes imbalanced in the nutrient tank.

In order to reduce the pH of the standard nutrient solution the bicarbonate ions have to be neutralized. Because these alkaline ions buffer the solution it is necessary to add large amounts of Phosphoric acid to the nutrient in order to reduce the pH. This in turn increases the Phosphate ion content of the solution causing an imbalance. This imbalance can have serious consequences for your plants in a very short period of time.

What can I do about it?

The simplest way around the problem is to use a nutrient formulated specifically for hard water areas. A Hard Water nutrient has been produced with the correct balance of nutrients to compensate for the excess alkaline mineral ions in the water. These nutrients are also much more acidic to combat the buffering action of the bicarbonates.

The benefit of using this formulation is that you will not have to add large amounts of adjusting chemicals to your nutrient in order to achieve the correct pH. Also your plants will have a balanced nutrient solution containing all the ingredients they require to thrive. This means that your crop will grow up healthy with better growth and a superior yield.

HISTORY

The History and Potential Uses of Hydroponics

Hydroponics is the science of growing plants without soil. History shows us that this is by no means a new concept. In ancient times the hanging gardens of Babylon, the floating gardens of the Aztecs of Mexico and those of the Chinese were all early examples of 'Hydroponic' culture. Egyptian writings dating back to several hundred years before Christ have descriptions of the growing of plants in water.

During the 1930s, scientists experimenting with the growing of plants without soil, using nutrients dissolved in water, discovered that the soil was needed only as an anchor for the plant's root system. Since that time more and more research has resulted in the development of commercial nutrients and purpose built systems of differing types. Hydroponics is now popular in Western Europe, Australia, Canada and many other areas of the world.

As technology advances more and more of the world's food is produced using hydroponic methods. Although rooted in history, it is still a relatively young science, Hydroponics has progressed rapidly over the past half century, it has been adapted to suit many and varied situations from outdoor farming to greenhouse production and now also indoor home cultivation. The military use it for growing fresh vegetables in submarines and the space programs are even experimenting with Hydroponics to feed the crews on board manned space stations The potential use of Hydroponics for future cultivation is enormous. It is already being looked at for increasing the food production in underdeveloped countries where space can be a factor. Because it is feasible to grow in areas of poor and even barren soil, arid regions of the world such as deserts could be utilized to grow crops hydroponically. The desert sand could be used as an ideal growing media and the nutrients even mixed with sea water, once the salts have been removed.

Even in countries with a more temperate climate Hydroponics can be used for food production, the temperature being maintained with the use of modern grow lights.

In Holland and other European countries, the production of vegetables, such as Lettuce and fruits, like Tomatoes is showing that Hydroponic methods can be very effective and cost efficient. A large proportion of this produce is now being grown that way.

Some 20 plus years ago racehorse stables in the U K were looking at production of highly nutritious barley and wheat 'grass' as a feed. It was then very expensive and in its infancy, however today a large number of horse owners feed their animals in this way. It is also not unheard of for farmers to use the same methods to feed their cattle during the winter periods when the fields are too wet to graze.

With the advent of more efficient methods of production the uses of soil-less culture will advance and multiply as more people experiment with the systems available.

NUTRIENTS

How well do you know your nutrients?

There are many different plant nutrients on the hydroponics market today. Their function is to provide the optimum mix of Nitrogen, Phosphorous, Potassium, Calcium and various other trace elements, in order to sustain growth, improve yields and allow the plant to achieve its potential. The plants requirements will vary to some extent as it develops. Concentrations and plant food components may also vary with differing growing mediums. The food is absorbed through the plants roots and transported to the leaves, where it is converted into the sugars that the plant needs for energy.

The most important thing to remember about plant nutrition is that the NPK, (Nitrogen, Phosphorous, Potassium) Calcium and trace element ratios are correct. There can be a wide variation of ingredients in the various mixes for sale.

Because the plant will take whatever it requires from the elements available and leave the rest, the balance will alter as unused elements build up in the solution. If left unchecked this will result in a toxic buildup of salts and a subsequent drop off in growth followed eventually by the death of your, well-loved and nurtured, plants. This same result will occur if the water content is not replaced and the mixture strength increases. If the plant transpires 50% of the water from the supply tank, the concentration of elements within the solution will become dangerously high.

The concentration of salts in the feeding solution is measured using an Electrical Conductivity (EC) meter. The EC meter measures the strength of the solution in parts per million. This means that in a 1000 PPM solution there are 1,000 units of dissolved salts to every 1,000,000 units of water. The meter measures the total salt concentration in solution and does not discriminate between Potassium salts say and Calcium salts. It cannot tell the difference between a good and a bad mix, only their relative strengths.

The EC meter works by measuring the speed at which electrons travel between probes immersed in a solution. In distilled water, the electrons cannot find any impurities to use as footholds to cross the water and so the meter returns a 0 reading in mMho or mS (these are units used to measure electrical conductivity). As food is added to the water, the concentration of impurities in the form of salts increases and the electrons can find more footholds, and so cross the water faster. Thus the meter reading rises. Of course this is a very simplified explanation, but it should serve to give you an idea of the basics. One other important thing to remember is that as in all things chemical temperature plays an important part. The higher the temperature, the faster the electrons move and the higher the EC reading. This means that

that in order to accurately assess your mixture's EC you must record the PPM as mMho (mS) at a specific temperature.

As the PPM reading is a conversion from an electrical reading and as each addition of a different salt will alter the electrical properties, in order to obtain an accurate EC reading you will have to use a reference solution of a known value. Because the EC meter you are using will not necessarily have been calibrated for the mix used by the people who prepared your reference solution, these values can be quite inaccurate. In view of this, any reference solution that does not show the EC value in mS, or give you the conversion ratio that was used, is of no use for nutrient evaluation purposes.

It is important to note that if the nutrient EC reaches 3,000 PPM (or the meter reads over 4.0mS) your plants will begin to show signs of nutrient deficiency even though they will have an excess. The reasons for this are quite complex, but basically it is because the chemicals dissolved in the solution are competing for the available water and the stronger ones are blocking out some of the weaker ones. This leads to the roots having to work harder to absorb the nutrients. By working harder, they have to expend more energy at the expense of growth. If at this time the temperature rises and the water level drops, due to evaporation, your plants will, very probably, die.

Probably the most important factor that will affect your plant growth in relation to nutrient uptake is pH. Different types of plant prefer different pH values and it is important to ascertain which the optimum for the species you are growing is. The medium in which you are growing will affect the cation exchange capacity of the plant. This is the ability of the medium to hold nutrients on call for the plant roots to use. Normal soil has a high cation exchange rate (CEC) of between 100 and 200 equivalent units. A number of growing mediums and of course water cultures have a CEC of 0. This means that once a nutrient has passed the roots it cannot be taken up by the plant, and neither will it have any buffering effect. The nutrients, the gasses, the trace elements, the water and the growing medium all have differing electrical charges and are all exchanging positive and negative charges around the roots of the plant. This ionic battle enables the roots to absorb the nutrients it needs to sustain the plant. If the pH is incorrect it stops the particle exchange. This is because the shapes and sizes of the charged particles will be different from the spaces available within the plant root tissue. The pH can be looked at a bit like a Yale lock and key. If all is correct the lock opens if the plant pH and the surrounding pH differ then the lock cannot open.

Different plants need different nutrients at differing stages of their growth. These nutrients have different charges and so in order to get the greatest nutrient uptake the pH must be closely monitored. If in doubt about the requirements of your plant try asking the manufacturer of your nutrients for help. After all he made the mix in the first place and so should know all there is to know about it.

If your plants are not thriving look at the pH as the primary cause and try to work out which of the nutrients is not being absorbed and why.

pH

pH Is The Most Important Factor In Aquaculture.

What Is pH?

pH is the term used to assess the acidity or alkalinity of a solution. This acidity or alkalinity is determined by measuring the concentration of Hydrogen ions in the solution. This normally falls between 10 0 and 10-14 gram-equivalents per litre. In order to simplify this, a scale of values between 0 and 14 has been adopted.

This pH scale is a measurement of how strongly the electrical charges hold the atoms and molecules of substances within the solution together. The higher the concentration of positively charged ions, the lower the value is on the scale and the higher the concentration of negatively charged ions the greater the pH value.

Hydrogen (H+) has a positive charge while the hydroxides (OH-) have a negative charge. Pure water has a value of 7.0 so it is easy to see that water must be H-OH or more commonly H2O.

The decimal points on the scale are very important because each whole number is approximately 10 times greater (or less) than the next whole number. So pH 2.0

is 1000 times stronger than pH5. The greater the concentration of Hydrogen ions in the solution the more acidic it is said to be and the lower its pH on the scale. The greater the number of hydroxide ions the greater the alkalinity (or basicity) it is said to have and the higher its pH.

If we look at the structure of the pH scale, we can see that it goes from 0 (very strong acid) to 7 (neutral) and then to 14.0(very strong Base or Alkali). If we mix an acidic solution with an alkaline one, providing that the positions on the scale are equidistant from the neutral value of 7.0, we will end up with a neutral solution. This is because the positive charges will be cancelled out by the negative ones. If however we use differing positions on the scale, then the resulting imbalance will give us a solution with either acidic or basic properties depending on which side had the greater distance from the neutral value.

But Why Is This So Important?

All of the chemicals in the solution have differing electrical charges because each of them is made up of different combinations of elements and ionic values. As they are all competing for the exchange of charged particles, a huge electrical battle is constantly raging within the solution. This constant exchange of positive and negative charges surrounds the plant's root system and it is this that allows it to absorb the vital nutrients needed for its growth.

You can think about the chemical battle being a bit like a moving 3D jigsaw puzzle, with the positive and negative charges all having to combine in the correct shape and order. The plant can only absorb those bits that fit into its own bits, like a lock and key. As the levels of pH change, so the jigsaw bits alter and no longer open the lock. In fact the plant itself will, at times, alter its own internal cellular pH in order to either slow down or speed up certain enzyme reactions.

It is vitally important that the pH of the nutrient used in the hydroponic system matches the plant's own internal pH as closely as possible, otherwise this chemical exchange cannot take place. The main chemicals within the solution, Sodium ($Na+$), Phosphorous ($P+$), Calcium ($Ca+$) and Potassium ($K+$), together with all the other elements will affect the efficiency of each nutrient's absorption through the root walls.

Different species of plant prefer different pH values. The three main things that affect the pH that a plant prefers are:

1 The pH of the water used.

Your water will not be pure and so will contain charged ions either from deliberately introduced contaminants or from environmentally absorbed ones like Calcium

Carbonate from passing through limestone and Sulphurs from acid rain.

2 The growing medium that you are using.

Rockwool is over pH 7.0, Peat Moss below 6.0 and hardened expanded clay is 7.59.

3 The nutrient you are using.

Nutrients can be mixed in lots of different ways, forming various combinations of elements and so giving a wide variation in pH. Because these chemical combinations behave in different ways they give up their elements to the plant at differing pH values. Therefore, the nutrient preferred by the plant determines which the best pH value for that species is.

H_2O_2

Hydrogen Peroxide (H_2O_2) is a water molecule with an extra atom of Oxygen attached ($2H_2O + O_2 = 2H_2O_2$). This extra Oxygen atom is quite easily detached from the water molecule and eagerly combines with any suitable substance that has the room for it. For example, it will attack organic blood cells.

Any chemist's shop will sell you some concentrated 35% Hydrogen Peroxide, which may be diluted with water to give a 3% solution for human use. This diluted solution is good for treating minor cuts and scrapes etc. It is also used for softening ear wax. It works by oxidizing the chemical parts that are presenting as having a free space for the Oxygen atom.

When H_2O_2 comes in contact with these "impurities" it will give a reaction which causes it to fizz. This fizzing is the Oxygen atoms coming out of their bond with the water molecules and bubbling out of the solution. As gardeners, we can use this eagerness to break its bond to help keep our plants free from everyday pests.

In the same way as old organic blood cells are attacked and consumed by the fizzing action of the peroxide, so will any bacteria and small insects be destroyed by a solution of up to 5% H_2O_2. At this strength it is safe for human skin but lethal to most bugs.

Mix up the following for a weekly preventative spray:

• Add to 1Litre of Water:

• 30ml of 35% Hydrogen Peroxide

• 20 ml of Alcohol (Old style mouth wash works well)

• 2ml of wetting agent (Washing up liquid will do)

• Use this mixture as a foliar spray to keep your plants healthy and free from bugs.

Another advantage of the Peroxide breaking down is that it releases free Oxygen into the area. So, if you were to add some to your nutrient tank, the dissolved Oxygen being released around the root system not only kills any bad root material and bacteria, but also oxygenates the roots with the excess Oxygen produced.

Plants can easily cope with a 5% H_2O_2 solution and because the mixture reduces to water in a short space of time, the dilutions are not that critical. For this reason, it also makes a great disinfectant for plant pots, greenhouses and grow-rooms.

It may be used at 10% for these jobs, but make sure to only use it if the area is plant free. A really great advantage is that you do not have to rinse it away after use because it will revert to water on its own.

CO_2

How Carbon Dioxide (CO_2) Can Keep Your Plants Growing!

Carbon, Hydrogen and Oxygen make up about 90% of the dry matter in a plant. CO_2 (Carbon Dioxide) in the air supplies all of the Carbon in the plant. Like animals, plants breathe in Oxygen and breathe out Carbon Dioxide all the time. The plant needs Carbon Dioxide during the hours of daylight and uses this to produce sugars. During the hours of darkness, it will breathe out Carbon Dioxide, which is a waste product.

The plant uses light and Carbon Dioxide for photosynthesis. The more light there is available the greater the plant's requirement for Carbon Dioxide, It has been found that it takes about 10 photons, (quantum units of light) during photosynthesis, to create enough energy to split one Carbon Dioxide molecule into its basic components of Carbon and Oxygen and form a sugar.

Because there are trillions of photons hitting the plant's leaves, sufficient Carbon Dioxide is needed to convert their energy into sugars. If enough CO_2 is not available, then the unused photons will bounce off the plant's leaves and be lost. So the more the light the plant is given the more Carbon Dioxide it will need to produce its maximum yield of sugars from photosynthesis.

Plants absorb different spectrums of light in differing amounts. This light is affected in different ways by a range of factors, such as distance and percentage of reflection etc. Because any unusable light is wasted, the calculation of how much useable light the plant is getting is quite complicated. It can be measured using a special PAR meter (PAR = Photosynthetically Active Radiation).

This machine takes into account the lumen level of the light striking the leaves and discounts the unusable fractions of the available light.

Plants outside, in full sunlight, will get about 5000 lumens per square foot. This means that the plant could process about 2000 ppm of CO_2. It is unfortunate that the Carbon Dioxide levels outside are nowhere near this level.

Indoors, using a light level of 3000 lumens, the plant will need approximately 1500 ppm of CO_2. If the light level was at 1000 lumens this would drop to around 300 ppm CO_2 (city air is about 400 ppm) which is within the normal range. The lower the concentration of Carbon Dioxide the more the air has to be moved across the plant's leaves in order for it to get sufficient exchange.

It is known that if the plant has enough CO_2 and enough light it will perform to its optimum, so if we increase the light levels and up the CO_2 available then we can expect a good increase in growth and subsequent yield.

OXYGEN

How Oxygen Keeps Your Plants Thriving!

Oxygen is used in large quantities by plants. If you were to analyze a dried plant you would find that about 45% consisted of Oxygen atoms. Just like humans, plants need fresh air and their cells use Oxygen in the same kind of quantities that ours do. In air conditions with a low concentration of Oxygen, or where the air is poor, plants do not thrive. Those that do manage to eke out an existence remain poor stunted specimens.

The leaves of a plant have easy access to Oxygen. They make it as a natural bi-product of the process of producing plant sugars

and breathe it out as waste during the process of photosynthesis.

The roots of the plant do not have the same amount of Oxygen available to them. They have to work a lot harder to find enough for their needs. Insufficient Oxygen at the roots will reduce the plants root respiration and result in the shutting down of photosynthesis.

A plant's growth and its yield are governed by the size and health of its root system. It can only grow to its full potential if the roots have enough Oxygen for their needs. In plants grown hydroponically this essential ingredient is supplied dissolved in the nutrient solution.

Dissolved Oxygen in the nutrient solution can be measured by a DO meter. These are available from all good hydroponics equipment suppliers.

The amount of Oxygen dissolved in the solution will vary depending on both temperature and pressure. The warmer the water the lower the gaseous content will be. Really cold fresh water has a DO reading of up to 14 ppm or 14mg/litre, while water at 30 degrees centigrade can only hold about 5ppm or 5 mg/l DO.

This DO only amounts to a very small percentage of the roots needs. All water culture systems have to utilize some other form of oxygenation for the roots as well as DO in the nutrient. Root systems that have insufficient Oxygen available will soon turn brown and become very sick.

We aerate the nutrient in our systems in order to get the best saturation that we can, (from 5ppm to 8ppm) but the main function of this aeration is to kill off the anaerobic bacteria around the roots. Anaerobic bacteria are pathogens that cannot survive in an oxygenated environment; (Anaerobic meaning without air).

Because the dissolved Oxygen in the nutrient can only supply about 1% of the roots requirements, the balance must be made up by breathing air. This air is trapped within the soil in conventional gardening and in the growing medium in normal hydroponics systems. This Oxygen search uses up energy that the plant could better use to produce root growth.

The only type of system where this does not happen is the aeroponics system. The aerated water being sprayed directly onto the roots, allows the plant to take in free Oxygen from the surrounding air, while still keeping the roots moist and supplied with nutrient.

One of the functions of Oxygen is to facilitate the exchange of nutrients and gasses between the plant roots and the surrounding solution. It does this by changing the electrical charges within the water, so allowing the roots to absorb the available nutrients with the least expenditure of energy. For this reason, if no other, the roots need all the Oxygen they can get.

OZONE

The Uses And Dangers Of Ozone (O3) In The Grow Room

Ozone or Trivalent Oxygen (O3) is an unstable gas made up of three Oxygen atoms. It is formed when a single Oxygen atom attaches itself to an Oxygen molecule (O2). Ozone is very unstable and will revert back to Oxygen very easily, (2O3 = 3O2).

Because this third atom is so easily dislodged from the molecule, it will freely combine with any other molecule that has a spare space for it.

This process of is called Oxidation and is the reason why Ozone is an excellent killer of bacteria, moulds and viruses. It is also an effective means of removing odors, which it does by attaching to the scent molecule and altering its chemical makeup. This does not mask the smell; it destroys it at source.

Ozone is produced naturally in two ways; Firstly, by the chemical reaction with the sun's Ultra Violet rays in the upper atmosphere and secondly by Corona-Discharge.

For most practical applications Ozone is generated using the Corona-Discharge method.

In nature, when there is a thunderstorm, massive voltages are passed through the air as the lightning jumps from cloud to Earth. This electrical discharge with its accompanying blue/white corona causes some of the Oxygen Molecules to break down from O_2 to $2O$ which in turn immediately attaches to another 2 Oxygen molecules giving the equation $2O_2 + 2O = 2O_3$. This also happens when the energy produced by very heavy rain and waterfalls causes the natural production of Ozone.

Because any impurities in the air around us, for example exhaust fumes, will have been cleansed by the Ozone molecule combining with them and then reverting to pure Oxygen and oxidized pollutants, which are virtually odorless, the air will smell clean and fresh. So the advantages of using O_3 as a means of providing your plants with extra Oxygen are several: The increased Oxygen levels, the odor control, and the anti-microbial and spore controlling properties.

Ozone generators can be purchased from most reputable Hydroponics suppliers. These work by passing Oxygen through a strong UV light or, more commonly, by using a high voltage discharge to break down the Oxygen molecules. In practice the UV system produces considerably less O_3, per unit of energy used, than does the Corona-Discharge method.

There has been a lot of discussion about the dangers associated with Ozone in confined spaces. Ozone has a strong recognizable odor, so very low concentrations soon become apparent. This makes it generally safe to work with. The use of Ozone is thought to be safe in low

levels (0.05ppm); however, in higher concentrations it can be very dangerous. Because it oxidizes materials readily it can cause severe irritation to lung tissue and mucous membranes. Other symptoms include headache and a feeling of tightness in the chest, coughing and dryness in the mouth and throat.

Recommended safe levels of maximum acceptable concentration (MAC) for humans are: 0.06 ppm for 8 hours per day 5 days per week (ppm = parts per million). For a maximum of 15 minutes a MAC value of 0.3 ppm may be applied. These levels far exceed that where the gas is noticeable by smell.

While it is quite possible and fairly easy to make an Ozone generator at home please bear in mind that a good working knowledge of high voltage electricity and its associated safety procedures is essential to avoid injury or even death.

It is always better to spend a little extra money on a resource and know that it is safe for you and your family to be around, rather than risk a less safe alternative which could end in a tragedy.

TEMPERATURE

Take Control of Your Grow Room Temperature

It is vital to maintain a temperature within the specified upper and lower limits for the species of plant being grown. This temperature may need to vary between dark and light periods, again dependent upon species. The desired results are usually obtained by either fans, to lower the ambient room temperature, or heat sources to raise it.

Reducing the room temperature can be done in various ways. For example, if your grow room is quite small and the air input via say a 4-inch diameter ducting system, then you might decide to use another slightly larger duct with an in-line fan to extract

the warm air and send it to the outside atmosphere. This can be supplemented by the use of free standing oscillating fans circulating the grow room air. Should more cooling be needed, in some hot climates for example, then an air cooler can be used. This can be easily made by passing the air over a refrigerated surface like a car radiator with ice cold water running through it.

It goes without saying that when the lights are turned off the temperature will reduce quite rapidly. If your grow room is not very well insulated, this is when you may need to turn on your heaters. Most growers find that it is more efficient to increase the insulation to a point where the heat loss is minimal, rather than spend money on raising the ambient temperature too much.

It is important to remember that any heat source used must not be placed so close to the plants as to burn them. Oil filled radiators and similar systems can be used with good effect.

In order to monitor the system some kind of sensor and switching device will be needed. These control systems are readily available at most suppliers. You will need a sensor for temperature linked to a switch for powering the cooling systems. Do not however rely upon them to never fail. I know of growers who have left their plants unattended for several days, only to return to a dead crop of nearly mature plants. The culprit being

a defunct control unit that allowed the lights to stay on and did not turn on the fans when the temperature climbed.

It is always wise to monitor your plants on a regular daily basis.

GERMINATION

Many advantages are to be gained over conventional, soil based, seed germination, by using hydroponics. The growing mediums are clean and in a lot of cases sterile, which reduces the instances of disease and infection, as well as insect attack. Soil may contain all kinds of harmful bacteria, fungal spores and insects that might harm vulnerable young plants. Root rot should also be easily avoided, using a high quality growing medium.

Because the hydroponics gardener has complete control over the plant's environment, it is possible to ensure that each and every aspect of the plant's growth is catered for to its optimum effect. This, of course, rules out the inconsistencies in the weather and avoids problems such as late frosts and storms etc. The subsequent advantage to the plants is an ideal climate in which to grow strong and healthy. This leads, eventually, to greater and better quality yields.

A lot of seeds contain their own nutrients and require only water and Oxygen in order to sprout. It is important to realize that using a nutrient solution can and often will either retard or block the seed's ability to germinate. Once it has sprouted and has reached a point where it has viable leaves, then it can be fed using a weak nutrient solution. One species of plant that has very little nutrient within the seed is the Orchid, so, as you can see, it is important to research your plants prior to germination in order to minimize any stress to the plant.

The choice of growing medium is important when dealing with seedlings and young clones. It must provide the young plant with water and Oxygen in adequate quantities, while not allowing it to become waterlogged. Drainage is very important at this time and the porous growing mediums have excellent properties in this area.

Perlite, Vermiculite and Rockwool all offer great drainage properties together with the major advantage, in the case of Rockwool, of coming in nice little cubes with holes in for your seeds. The beauty of these cubes is that they can be transplanted straight into larger Rockwool cubes or other mediums as the seedling grows, thus cutting down on the plant's stress and on the transplanter's time.

It is better to plant the germinated seeds in a medium with a built in weak nutrient and to add water only. When the seedlings are established you can then start them in a weaker version of your normal nutrient and gradually increase the strength until you are running at normal strength nutrient. This system can be ongoing, with germinating seeds being brought on at regular intervals to replace plants that have reached their fruiting stage and been cropped.

SOIL BASED

Why choose hydroponics over the conventional gardening methods using soil and composts etc.? There are several reasons for considering hydroponics or Aquaculture and these are listed below.

Time The most obvious benefit of Hydroponics is the saving in time and effort. You do not have to spend as much time attending to the preparation and maintenance of your garden on a regular basis, so a simple Aquaculture system can be much more time efficient than a conventional soil based one.

Weeds Growing in soil involves keeping your planting area weed free. In order to give your plants the best possible chance of thriving, they must be able to absorb their optimum nutrition from the surrounding soil. If the area has lots of weeds then your plants have to fight for their place, their roots competing with those of all the weeds. In the Hydroponics Garden, because the growing medium is sterile, there should not be any weeds appearing. This means that your plants can devote all their energy to production and not have the stresses of competition.

Health No soil and sterile growing media coupled with the correct nutrients means healthier plants. The absence of parasites and pathogenic bacteria in the growing media ensures that your plant roots stay healthy and disease free. Any infections or pests above ground can be monitored and treated quickly and efficiently because the growing area is more compact.

Light Outside, in the conventional garden, the sunlight is never predictable in either intensity or duration. Inside, under lights you have complete control and can supply your plants with a constant unchanging environment.

Growth Optimum nutrition and water requirements having been satisfied, your hydroponically grown plants will develop a massive but compact root system. This means that your plant will not have to use extra energy either searching for sustenance or transporting nutrients and sugars long distances. The net result of this is quicker growing, faster maturing and greater yielding plants.

Stress Your plants will not be stressed through changes in conditions of light, temperature or water as is the case with plants grown by the conventional gardening methods. This in turn will lead to stronger more resistant plants.

Yielding Your plants will yield considerably greater crops than conventionally grown ones because of all of the above factors. The greater storage capacity within the root system and the shorter stems give rise to an increase in plant efficiency of up to %30, with a corresponding increase in crop.

Cleanliness Hydroponics Gardening is in essence a clean occupation. There is no soil, so very little dirt. For this reason, it is ideal for indoor gardening, utilizing the spare room, or perhaps a conservatory. On top of this there are no more grime encrusted fingernails!

DISEASE

Plants, like animals are vulnerable to disease. All living things are made up of a collection of cells. Plant and animal cell structure is similar in makeup, having a cell wall containing the cell's internal components, such as the nucleus and the protoplast: the 'hollow' part of the cell where the cell conducts activities. There are many different types of plant cell, but all cells, be they plant or animal, share some basic characteristics.

Because they are cellular structures, plants are subject to disruption of their cells by invading organisms. Thus at the microbial level the plant may be invaded by pathogens. These are organisms which do harm or cause the death of the plant by extracting its nutrients, damaging the cell structure, or producing toxic by-products. These pathogens can come in the form of either viruses or bacteria. Both of these types of infection will do major harm to your carefully nurtured plant.

Bacteria attack the plant cells in the same way that they attack our own cells. Think back to the last time you had a cold or flu, remember how unwell you felt and how your energy was depleted. The plant also has to use a lot of energy in order to stop infection from spreading. One way in which it can fight back is by sealing off the diseased area and so blocking the pathways available to the intruding pathogen.

It has been found that plants also use Salicylic Acid (the active ingredient in aspirin) as a trigger to mobilize their defenses against attack.

Unfortunately, as there are no antibiotics that can be used on plants, the pathogenic bacteria are very difficult, if not impossible, to kill. They normally enter the plant via the site of some type of injury. For this reason, if no other, it is very important to check your plants daily for signs of damage from insects and other predation, as well as physical cuts and scratches.

Virus attack is usually caused in a similar manner, but these organisms are very much smaller than bacteria and can enter via the tiniest mark. Once inside the plant they live within the cells and are unable to be killed without destroying the plant.

Plants are also susceptible to fungal infections. Fungi, unlike the microbial pathogens, attack using spores. These can lie dormant for long periods of time and then be triggered to come to life. They are mainly an essential and welcome addition to the garden because they break down dead and decaying material and improve the humus content of the soil. Some, however, are bad news for the grower and cause disease within the growing area.

Fungi in general tend to attach to the outside of the plant and use root like structures to penetrate the plant and steal its nutrients. For this reason, they are vulnerable to chemical attack and destruction. There are various preparations available for eradicating fungal attack.

The best form of defense against plant disease is vigilance and meticulous hygiene. Here are a few ways in which you can help to prevent attack within your grow room or greenhouse.

Always wash your hands in hot soapy water before entering the growing area.

Always destroy diseased plants and all their dead leaves and debris.

Always use new, or well washed and sterilized, pots when planting new plants and cuttings.

Always sterilize your secateurs and equipment before use. This can be done by dipping the blades in Methylated Spirit, shaking off any excess and then lighting it. Care must be taken not to either ignite the alcohol bottle or burn the user or equipment. If you wish, you can just dip them in the spirit and allow it to dry. The use of a naked flame on knife blades etc is recommended when taking cuttings.

Allow as much free air between your plants as possible. This cuts down on the transmission of fungal infections.

Ban all smokers from your growing area. Tobacco is one of the biggest causes of the spread of Tobacco Mosaic Virus which attacks various plants. It is carried on the skin of people who use tobacco products.

Finally, always be on the lookout for changes in your plant's appearance. This can be the early sign of a disease.

AUXINS

Auxins Start Your Plant's Growth, Top and Bottom

Auxins drive the plant's shoots and roots to thrive, they are primarily concentrated in the root and shoot endings. Produced mainly in the buds and leaves of the plant, they promote the elongation of plant cells. The greatest concentrations are found in the root and shoot tips because the greater the concentration of Auxins, the better the growth of the root and shoot will be.

New roots need Auxins to get started and the shoots tips need them to sustain continued growth. In cuttings this hormone must be redeployed from the shoots to the root beginnings so that the roots can start to grow. Artificial rooting and shooting powders and gels are often used to boost the hormone levels during this process.

It is essential to always use the weakest possible rooting powder or gel. The reason for this is that too great a concentration of Auxins will actually stop the roots from developing. The rooting compound must all be gone within a few days, so this is a definite case of less being more.

One strange thing, which is, as yet, unexplained is the gravitation of the Auxins to the underside of a horizontal branch or stem. This causes the cells on the underside to elongate faster than those on the upper surface, resulting in the stem or branch curving upwards until the vertical is almost achieved and the greatest light is accessed.

On occasions a cutting taken from a horizontal branch will not grow upwards even as it gets older. It is thought that in this instance the cutting of the donor stem has disrupted the message sent by the growth hormone.

Another unexplained anomaly is the action of the Auxins on the shaded side of the plant's shoots. This accumulation of hormone causes the shady side to elongate more than the lighted side and so making the shoot curve towards the light.

The Auxins also accumulate in the top section of the growing shoots, causing the plant to grow upwards towards the light. The main shoots will grow at a quicker rate than their companions. This is because they have the ability to slow the growth of the other shoots by altering the Auxin concentrations. As the dominant shoot grows away from its less dominant companions so its ability to affect them decreases and they can then start to catch up. Should the dominant main shoot be broken or pinched out the Auxins within will be redistributed amongst the other shoots. These shoots will then start to grow stronger.

GIBBERELLIN

Gibberellins Awaken the Plant's Seeds and Control Internodal Length.

Gibberellins primarily develop in the plant's shoots, buds and seeds. They are involved in breaking the cycle of dormancy in the seeds and in the process of seed growth signals. They promote extra length and fast growth of cells between the plant's nodes and in the leaves. It is these hormones that are responsible for driving the plant rapidly upwards, making it long and spindly, in low light conditions.

The shorter the distance between the nodes of a plant, (the point from which each leaf shoots) the more efficient the plant will be in relation to its root size. This is because the taller it is the more energy it will need to use for growing the thicker, longer, stems needed to hold the extra weight. Also it will use more energy to transport its water and plant sugars over the greater distances from roots to leaves.

Another reason in indoor plants is that the taller the plant is the steeper the angle of shade becomes making a greater space necessary for its neighboring plants.

Artificial light halves in intensity for each foot from the source, meaning the leaves at the bottom of the plant are getting weaker light than those at the top. The taller the plant grows the further away the lamp must be placed and so the weaker still the light intensity impinging on the bottom layers.

A final drawback with tall plants is that the CO_2 needed by the plant will tend to collect at the lower levels because it is heavier than air. This will make getting it to the upper levels more difficult and of course, ultimately, costlier.

It is obviously better to limit the height growth and increase the potential yield gained by this action. The Gibberellins within the plant will slow the growth of the stem cells under good light levels. Increase the light intensity and the growth will be transferred from height to root ball and plant density. Remember, the more root and leaves, the more flowers, fruit and seeds.

The complicated interaction of Auxins and Gibberellins is responsible for the way in which the plant reacts to the available light. The Auxins make it turn towards the brighter light while the Gibberellins slow its growth when the optimum light intensity is reached. Outside, in the sunshine, this is a very delicate and complex interaction as the light varies from day to day and month to month.

There are in excess of 70 different types of Gibberellins that assist in the germination of seeds, the elongation of stems and leaves and also affect the development of fruit.

Auxin-Gibberellin sprays are used by commercial growers to promote the growth of some fruits such as apples, currants and eggplants without fertilization. An example of one interesting use for Gibberellins is in the production of the Thompson variety of seedless grapes.

CYTOKININS

Cytokinins Influence How Fast and How Often Your Plant's Cells Divide

Cytokinins are organic chemical compounds containing Carbon, Hydrogen and Nitrogen, whose structure resembles that of Adenine. They promote cell division and have other similar functions to Kinetin, which was the first cytokinin discovered and named because of its ability to promote cytokinesis (cell division).

Despite being a natural compound, Kinetin is not made by plants, which leads to it being thought of as a "synthetic" Cytokinin. (A hormone synthesized somewhere other than in the plant.)

In today's plants the most common form of naturally occurring cytokinin is called Zeatin which was isolated from corn (Zea mays).

Cytokinins have been found in almost all higher plants as well as mosses, fungi, bacteria, and also in the RNA (definition) of many prokaryotes and eukaryotes. Today there are more than 200 natural and synthetic Cytokinins combined. Cytokinin concentrations are highest in meristematic regions.

Meristemic tissue is a type of cellular plant tissue containing non-specialised embryonic cells. It is found in areas of the plant where growth may take place, such as the shoots, buds and roots. Specialized plant cells have a precise set of rules that they follow in order to produce cells of the correct shape, size and structure. Because the plant needs to be adaptable as it grows it uses the meristemic cells in order to alter the shape and structure of the plant body as it grows.

Thus the meristem provides new cells which the plant uses to expand its basic body and form. This allows the plant to maintain its shape and type of structure according to its rules, while still giving leeway for growth. Each of the roots and shoots being able to grow and expand as needed throughout their lifetime.

Because this primary growth is not predetermined by the plant's blueprint, the overall shape of the plant is also indeterminate in advance. This gives each meristem the latent ability to develop into a complete plant. As a consequence of this new plants can be grown from cuttings where cells in the broken or cut end change to become specialized root cells. This method of reproduction is called Asexual or Vegetative Reproduction.

GENERAL SECRETS OF MASTER HYDROPONIC GROWERS

Starting and running a hydroponics garden may seem a daunting task but is actually a walk in the park. All you need is learn the basics and spend ample time fine-tuning your system. Once you have learned the fundamental concepts, set up your hydroponics garden, and have well-adjusted all elements and factors, then everything should be running smoothly.

The secret to hydroponics gardening is that "the food is in the water." Designing and setting up your system will focus and depend on this and the types of plants you intend to grow.

So read on to find out more about this secret.

Nutrients: The Perfect Mixture

Foods Your Plant Cannot Live Without

All plants require foods in the form of macronutrients and micronutrients to properly grow and bear the ideal yield. The same is true with hydroponics gardening.

The first group is composed primarily of nitrogen, phosphorous, and potassium and secondarily of calcium, magnesium, and sulfur. Some of the micronutrients needed by plants are boron, manganese, copper, zinc, chloride, iron, and molybdenum. In growing your favorite plant, it is a must that you use the perfect mixtures of nutrients that vary according to the particular growth stages they are in or else your investment in them will go down the drain.

These are the foods that your favorite plant needs in order to survive, yield the fruits you want in terms of quantity and quality, and grow healthy enough to reproduce:

Nitrogen: Plants need it in order to produce the proteins and enzymes that are used in photosynthesis and to enable the metabolism processes that are involved in it too. The healthy and right dosage of this nutrient will assure your fruit's quality of leaves and rapid seed production.

Phosphorous: It is primarily involved in the creation of oils and starches in plants. It aids in the transformation of energy from the sun into the much-needed chemical energy thus allowing your plant greater stress tolerance and proper maturation.

Potassium: It aids in protein building and ensures that plants have greater endurance against diseases.

Calcium: It makes the cell walls of plants stronger and provides greater strength to them.

Magnesium: It is essential to photosynthesis because it is a major part of chlorophyll.

Sulfur: This nutrient enhances the growth of plants and their resistance to cold weather.

Boron: It is an essential element in the production of seeds and fruits of plants.

Copper: It is an important ingredient in the reproduction processes of plants.

Zinc: This regulates plant growth. It produces auxin, which is and essential growth hormone. Zinc is also essential in the plant's root development and starch formation.

Iron: An ingredient in chlorophyll creation. Iron deficiency in plants can be minimized by choosing appropriate soil for the plant's growing conditions.

Molybdenum: It assists in nitrogen uses. This important nutrient is important in pollen formation.

Manganese: Assists in the breakdown of nitrogen and carbohydrates.

Magic Mixture Ratios Your Favorite Plants Would Love

Just like children, your favorite plants in your hydroponic garden need the right diet so that they will grow productive and healthy. Too much and too less of any of the nutrients will cause you problems that will cause you mental anguish and financial setbacks. You should take into consideration their growth stages before feeding them any mixture, which are the following:

Vegetative stage refers to that brief period of time where the plant begins photosynthesis. This also refers to the growth period where it develops its height, the thickness of the stems, would-be bud sites, and side branching.

Flowering or fruiting stage, which you will find very fulfilling, is the period when your plants will show their sex and bear flowers.

The 2:1:1 NPK Ratio

During the vegetative or growing stage in your hydroponic gardening, your plants should be fed a ratio of 2:1:1 nitrogen (N), phosphorous (P), and potassium (K). Here are some tips pertaining to the appropriate ratios that can be used during vegetative stage:

A ratio of 20:10:10. This would mean that 20% of the mixture should be composed of nitrogen, 10% should be phosphorous, 10% should be potassium, and the remaining 60% should be composed of secondary macronutrients and micronutrients.

A ratio of 30:15:15. This would require 30% of the mixture to be nitrogen, 15% phosphorous, and 15% potassium. The remaining 20% will be consisted of the secondary macronutrients and micronutrients.

These mix ratios will give your plants greater resources during photosynthesis and result to better quality of leaves and seeds.

The Flowering Mix

When your favorite plants begin to flower, adjust the ratio to 1:2:2 nitrogen, phosphorous, and potassium. There should be more phosphorous and potassium than nitrogen in the mix. If you use the 20:10:10 ratio during the growth stage, make use of 10:20:20 ratio during the flowering stage. And if you use the 30:15:15 ratio in the vegetative period, you must use the 15:30:30 ratio during the flowering period. With these ratios, your plants will become stronger and bear greater stress tolerance. Furthermore, it is even suggested that during the flowering stage in your hydroponic gardening project, you can stop feeding your plants with nitrogen and focus on phosphorous, potassium, magnesium, and sulfur. Overfeeding just like in the case of humans could kill.

10 Friendly Tips on Formulation and Feeding

There are two ways to procure the magic mixture and the right ratios. You either purchase pre-formulated nutrients or you formulate them on their own. In the first option, all you have to do is combine a standard quantity prescribed by the manufacturers of the concentrate with water. The second option though is the more cost-efficient and effective because your mixes will be based on what your plants would need. Whichever you choose, there are considerations that you must not forget such as the pH level or acid content of the formula because the ability of the roots to absorb the nutrients will depend on it. Here are some friendly tips you can peruse and consider:

Maintain your formulas' pH level at the best range for your favorite plants, which is 5.8 to 6.5. A level of pH at 1 is acidic, at 7 neutral, and 14 basic. You can measure the pH level by using a chemical test kit that needs replenishment because the materials are consumed or through electronic methods such as pens with LCD monitors that are dipped into the solution.

Adjust the ph level if necessary. This can be done by using distilled vinegar. A perfect mixture or balance among phosphoric, nitric, and sulfuric acids is important especially that they maximize the potential benefits that your plants could derive from nutrients such as phosphorous, nitrogen, and sulfur. In order to increase the pH base you can use potassium hydroxide and sodium hydroxides. You can use soda as an adjusting agent too.

Use alternative hydroponic systems in feeding the nutrients to the plants aside from those that are already in practice. Those systems that are most commonly used are aeroponics, continuous flow solution culture, static solution culture, flood and drain sub-irrigation, passive sub-irrigation, top irrigation, ultrasonic irrigation, and deep-water culture. Alternative feeding systems include the use of coconut fibers that are pre-treated. They have lesser potassium and sodium contents and are very rich with magnesium and calcium, which are both very useful in increasing or improving the growth of your plants.

Replace the nutrient solution at an interval of two weeks. Remove the old solution from the reservoir and clean the equipment with hot water to kill any unfriendly bacteria that could have been accumulated.

Recycle the old solution. Instead of throwing it away, use it to water the plants.

Maintain the level of the water reservoir. Be sure to check on it on a daily basis because water evaporates faster during hot days.

Do not overdo the feeding. Too much nutrient could lead to the death of your dear plants and would mean great losses on your part.

Dissolve the powdered solution before you place it in the water in the reservoir. If you are using concentrated liquids, better mix them before directly placing them into the water too.

Stop nutrient feeding your plants at least seven days prior to their harvest. Continue the water feeding though.

Oxygenate your water. You can age tap water for three days by placing it in a container.

Ventilation: Managing Heat

Due to the susceptibility of plants to weather changes, it is important that you manage heat well in your hydroponic garden. Some countries have only two seasons: wet and dry; and one of them is Australia. The dry seasons would usually last for six months where temperature is lower. During the wet seasons, which usually takes a period of six months too, there is too much rain and the temperature is high due to increased humidity in the air. For hydroponic growers like you, these weather changes could pose a lot of challenges because with the use of artificial lighting, natural temperature is heightened by the heat exuded by the artificial illumination. The more wattage you use, the greater heat is generated. Too much heat can kill your favorite plants even before they enjoy growth or flowering.

What You Can Do

There are several things that can be done to manage heat--to increase or decrease it. You must learn how to handle heat because they could either be too low or too high. If it is too low, your plants will die with cold; and with it too low their leaves will coil in and eventually die. These are some simple things you can do:

Use air-conditioners or vent systems to regulate airflow and thus the temperature of your hydroponics space. If air conditioners are too expensive for you in terms of electricity usage, then create a vent system. The most common vent systems are those that make hot air flow from the ceiling of your planting area to another room. Other vent systems are installed to exhaust the air through the chimney, walls, or even roofs. You can use simple equipment such as bathroom fans to serve as exhaust.

Monitor the humidity and temperature of your hydroponic growth area through a thermometer. Create a system that can clear up the heat in five minutes and in cycles of twenty-five minutes when the artificial lightings are turned on. You need a timer and fan for this type of system.

Set up a system that is based on thermostat. It will automatically turn a fan or air-conditioner on when a specific temperature or heat level is reached and will turn off the cooling equipment when the level decrease by at least 4 degrees Celsius.

For internal air movement purposes, oscillating fans will do. It will aid carbon dioxide circulation and at the same time will keep down the mounting humidity inside the garden. This is necessary to be done in order to reduce incidence of plant ailments due to fungus and absorb the moisture in the room.

To avoid declines in temperature, which usually takes place at night or when your artificial lighting is off, you should install a propane heater that is set to coordinate with a thermostat or timer. If you decide to use a thermostat, set it to detect a temperature fall below 20 degrees Celsius and to turn on the heater and to turn it off once the heat level is at 30 degrees Celsius. Furthermore, this system will provide your plants greater resources of carbon dioxide, which is an essential element in photosynthesis.

Installation of a thermo-hygrometer. You can switch it on for a period of twenty-four hours or longer. It will provide you accurate monitoring of the levels of humidity and temperature.

Lighting: Fluorescent and HPS

Light is needed by your favorite plant even in your hydroponic garden for photosynthesis and as indicators of weathers and seasons. With hydroponics lighting systems, you could control the time and duration of the exposure of the plants to light for purposes of standardizing the photosynthesis cycles. With them you could also simulate the seasons in order to encourage them to flower and extend the growing season so that you would enjoy year-round supply of your favorite plants and fruits. Imagine that even in seasons of winters, your plants would still continue to grow and prosper. If humans are provided calories by fats, plants get them from light. With artificial lighting, your favored plant could grow as high as six feet tall in three or four months.

Great Artificial Lighting Systems

Your favored hydroponic plant will surely bloom to its fullest potential and give you the best quality and quantity possible through the following artificial lighting systems:

Fluorescent and LED (or light emitting diodes) are best used during the stage where the seedlings of your plants are starting to grow.

Metal halide (or MH) and high pressure sodium (HPS) systems would be best for the flowering stage.

Fluorescent Bulbs Explained More

Fluorescent bulbs are ideal for seedlings, and because of their low intensity they need to be placed nearer the plants. They should be hanged at least eight to fifteen inches from the plants. They have the following benefits:

Enhancement of the health and strength of seedlings or cuttings

Superior root growth and quality

Maximize the plant response in terms of photosynthesis

Unveiling Metal Halide Bulbs

They provide your hydroponic garden abundant blue and green spectrum light, which is essential in the growth of the plants. With them, you can be assured that your plant's leaf growth would be maximized and they will grow sturdy or compact. Compared to fluorescent and incandescent bulbs, they are best for the flowering stage because their brightness is 125 lumens, which is quite enormous compared to the 18 lumens of incandescent and 39 lumens of fluorescent bulbs. They are both efficient and effective during the vegetative and flowering stages.

HPS Bulbs at Their Best

High pressure sodium bulbs are considered as best for the enhancement of the budding and flowering processes of your favored plants because they emit light of the red and yellow spectrum. In other words, they are bulbs emitting light that closely imitates natural light. Most users prefer them during the flowering stage of their hydroponic garden.

Basic Lighting Tips You Must Practice

Whatever your preferred system is for your hydroponic garden, you should not forget to do the following in order to maximize your plants' health, growth, and reproduction:

For two months, continuously expose the young plant or seedlings to light. When in vegetation stage, illuminate them at twenty-two hours in a day; and when they are flowering, keep them lighted at a maximum of twelve hours a day.

Keep the light close to the plants, but never allow them to touch even the leaves. When the edges of their leaves curl, it means that they are overheated.

During the vegetation stage, use bulbs that emit blue or red bands of the spectrum. Metal halide lamps provide the blue light; and fluorescent, the red light.

Minimum light exposure is twenty watts per foot. You can go much higher but not too high or else your plants may fry and not too low because they might droop.

Fix the lamps to the roof to afford you flexibility. As the plants grow taller, you can raise the bulbs higher.

Use reflectors to ensure uniform illumination among all your plants. Those that do not get sufficient light as the others would grow disfigured, taller, and thinner.

Plan and design a daily lighting cycle. If you will not do this, your plants will grow poorly. And if you wake them up when they already have been accustomed that it is the dark period of the day, they will be traumatized and could become ill.

Paint your walls, roofs, and even floors with white to provide greater light reflection capacity of your space. Brighten the days of your favorites and make them feel loved and cared for.

Clones: Increasing the Success Rate of Your Hydroponic Gardening

Cloning is simply taking a cutting from your growing plant and placing it together with other cuttings in a separate pot or container. Be sure that the clone you choose comes from female plants. When properly taken care of, they will become mature plants that are exact copies of the original or source plants. It is a method that would surely aid you in controlling the quality of your plants, seeds, and their fruits. The clones grow faster than those that are raised from seeds, and this will make your time usage more efficient.

Useful Tips to Improve Your Success Rates

Clones are very effective tools in reproducing your plants in your hydroponic project. You must take extra care though to ensure the success or else you will just be wasting time, energy, and money on them. These are useful tips that could help you:

Only clone plants that are healthy, well developed, and have enhanced flowering capabilities.

Take more cuttings than you need to plant so that you will have a wider range of choices. Choose among them the best.

Before taking a cutting, remove the nitrogen from the source plant by feeding it heavily with water that is pH adjusted and without any fertilizer or nutrient for at least two and maximum of three days. If you fail to do this, you will impede the growth of the roots of the clones.

Choose well the media that you will use for your clones. You can make use of cubes that are pre-formed and contain holes fit for the cuttings.

You should cut holes in the top of the medium that would be of the same size or circumference as the stems of your clones.

Take extra care when you cut. Do not forget to sterilize your cutting equipment before you proceed with the cloning process because you might infect the mother plant. Be sure that when you cut, you do it quickly in order to keep air from being shot into the stem.

The clone should be between three and six inches long--no more and no less. There should at least be one leaf inter-node and if possible, two inter-nodes.

Place the cuttings in a misting dome where they will be artificially moisturized two to three times in a day. Keep them well ventilated too by cutting small holes on the top of the dome. Maintain their temperature at 72 degrees to 80 degrees Fahrenheit.

Use double tube fluorescents that emit white light--both cold and warm. Keep them close to the clones at a distance of one or two inches. In case you use an artificial lighting system that utilizes metal halide bulbs or high pressure sodium lamps, keep the cuttings at a distance of two or three feet if the light source is between 175 and 400 watts. If the bulbs' wattage is at least a thousand, keep them at a distance of at least four feet. Keep the cuttings illuminated at least eighteen hours a day.

Water the clones every two days with distilled water with nutrients. If the external temperature is high, you can water them once a day. Do not make the mistake of submerging or setting them in water because the stems will become rotten or decayed.

In about a week, check on the clones. If you see that they have started to root, stop the misting or artificial moisturizing procedures. If they have properly rooted already, remove them from the dome and plant them.

Harvest: Curing the Correct Way

The Right Time to Harvest Your Hydroponic Garden

If you have reached as far as this, it only means one thing: you have been successful with your plants' growth and flowering stages. You have won over the challenges of hydroponic gardening and triumphantly circumvented the adversities of raising your beloved fruits. The average harvest time is after eight to twelve weeks of flowering. You must remember that they are best harvested when trichomes production or THC level is at a maximum. An indicator of this is when at least a third of their pistils or hairs have turned from white to dark such as brownish or reddish in color. Use a magnifying glass to monitor the pistils. Do not over-wait though until all of the pistils are dark because it will decrease the value of your plants.

Potency and quantity are two non-parallel objectives in harvesting. If the former is your goal, you should harvest when the THC level production is at its maximum and your harvested plants will weigh lesser but their quality would be a lot better. If the latter is your target, then harvest them after all the pistils are dark.

Drying to Improve Quality

After harvest, you have to separate the leaves from the buds. The next step would be to dry and cure them. You must not forget that your leaves and buds leave a bad taste in the mouth and have harsh aroma if they are used or consumed right after harvest. They must be dried to take out or evaporate the water from them. The curing step will complete the drying process and completely transform the leaves of your plants to bearers of good dreams and magic. Here are some things you must do when drying your plants:

Hang them in an environment that is dry, dark, and cool. Keep the temperature at 20 degrees Celsius or 68 degrees Fahrenheit. Too much heat and light will destroy their quality.

Do not directly handle the plants. Avoid damaging the quality of the heads, buds, and leaves by contaminating them with dirt or the sweat of your hands.

Separate the large branches and wider leaves in order for you to give better drying exposure to the smaller branches and narrower leaves.

Keep the drying branches at a distance of half a foot. When they are too close to each other, your plants might attract mold; and when they are too far from each other, they will be dried faster than what is necessary. Both situations will lead to the loss of potency and decrease in quality.

The average drying period is between a week and three weeks. To check if your plants have properly dried up already, take some branches and bend them. If they would snap at an angle of 90 degrees or less, it means that your plants are well dried already. If they will not, then you have to let them dry some more.

The Magic of Curing

Curing is an important procedure in your hydroponic gardening project as they are responsible for transforming your plants into marketable products with quality that is of high commercial values. Just be sure that before you do any of the steps related to curing, you have properly dried them. Observe the following tricks and for sure, you would enjoy the triumph that you have longed for:

Place in air-tight containers your plants. Store the containers in a room where the temperature is stabilized at 20 degrees Celsius. Be sure that no light will permeate the room because it will damage the product.

Any remaining moisture in the contents of the sealed containers will definitely evaporate and cling to the internal surface of the containers. Slowly open the lids and let the extra moisture escape. Do this during the first week at an interval of twenty-four hours for about a period of thirty minutes. During the second week, repeat the process at an interval of forty-eight hours. Repeat this in the third week and other succeeding weeks if necessary until all condensation is removed.

Watch out for possible decay caused by too much moist. Signs of decay include a smell that is the same to that of compost and new grass clippings.

Keep the dried plants that are not so green anymore stored in air-tight containers that should be placed in a place with a temperature of twenty degrees Celsius.

Keeping them in a fridge would help a lot in avoiding exposure to contamination, heat, and light that could cause deterioration of quality and shortening of shelf life. Keep them untouched for several weeks or months.

Prevention and Eradication

The prevention and eradication of bugs have been one of the most important concerns among hydroponic planters and scientists in agriculture. With the advent of more scientific researches and methods in studying bugs, modern science have come up with innovative methods to counter the growth and prevent the existence of bugs. The most recent and effective so far is biological pest control. This method is simple and only requires that friendly bugs are introduced to the environment to counter the damage of harmful bugs.

The Predator Bugs You Must Destroy in Your Hydroponic Garden

At different stages, your plant could suffer from different kinds of bugs. You should be familiar with them so that you will know how to prevent and destroy them. During the growth of the seedling of your plants the following bugs could infest them and either kill or damage them:

Cutworms: Larvae of the turnip moths. They feed on the leaves, stems, and buds of young seedlings.

Hemp flea beetles: They are very small jumping beetles that eat the leaves of seedlings.

Crickets: They are harmful to humans but very deadly to plants because they feed on leaves and buds, especially those that are just at their early growth.

When your plants grow taller and develop wider leaves and when they also start to flower, the following bugs would surely give you tons of headaches unless prevented:

Spider mites: They are very small and almost invisible to the human eyes. They reproduce at a very fast rate; and before you know it, they have destroyed your whole crop. The proof of their presence is usually the occurrence of dead spots on the leaves. When they have powerfully infested your plants, the leaves will turn yellow, almost the shade of bronze.

Aphids: They are also called plant lice and are very common in temperate zones. They feed on the sap of plants and are most likely to damage the flowers even before they bloom.

Whiteflies: They look like fruit flies but are more devious because they chew on the leaves and flowers of your dear plants.

Leafhoppers: Taxonomy wise, they are like grasshoppers just pretty smaller. They thrive on green leaves.

Other bugs that could infect the stems, stalks, and roots are the following:

European corn borers: They are generally found in corns, but they have also been observed to damage your favorite plants' stems.

Hemp borers: Most of the time they infest fruits, but they also love the stalks of your green healthy produce.

Weevils: They prefer dry plants or environment. They are dangerous destroyers of stalks and stems.

Root maggots: They feed on the roots of plants. They damage the osmosis capability of the roots.

Termites and ants: Self-organized insects that feed on the roots and are capable of adapting to whatever environment the plants are in.

Fungus gnats: They are dark small flies with short lives but vicious effect on the roots they infest.

The Best Solutions

There are many available solutions that would help you eradicate and prevent bug infestation of your favored plants. Five of these techniques are the following:

Biological pest control through the use of a beneficial or small animal that eats the bugs that damage your plants. They control adult pests and destroy their young, eggs, and larva. Some examples are predatory mites to counter greenhouse mites, nematodes for weevils, lace wing for aphids, and parasitic wasp for white flies.

Bio-best spray that either come in concentrates or spray cans. All you have to do is spray it on the affected leaves.

Sticky plates that serve as the alarm systems, and they draw bugs because of their yellow color.

Plant protectors that emit odors that are bug repellants.

Neem oil that damages the nervous systems of bugs.

Sound Preventive Measures

Eradication could be very expensive, and prevention could cost you nothing at all. Here are some suggestions that you may consider to prevent bugs infestations in your growth room:

Always clean your tools before and after using them.

Maintain proper drainage to ensure cleanliness of the area.

Do not overwater because the unused water can become the haven of bugs.

Quarantine infected plants to prevent others from being infested too.

The Perpetual Harvest: Sea of Green Techniques

These techniques involve the harvesting of batches of small plants that mature early. They refer to that method in hydroponic gardening where smaller plants are grown over shorter periods of time instead of growing few big plants over a long period of time. With hydroponics where the environment is controlled from lighting to ventilation, it is possible to start one batch at an earlier time, and as they mature, another batch is started. This method results to a year-round growing and harvesting cycle. Another way of doing this is starting all the plants together and creating a green canopy where you let your plant be harvested more times than once. Taller plants will be harvested from the top first without uprooting them. As the plant grows some more, the earlier lower level becomes the top that is ready for harvest.

9 781803 031699

Printed by BoD™in Norderstedt, Germany